Practice Book: Units 5–8

NATIONAL GEOGRAPHIC

Reach for Reading

COMMON CORE PROGRAM

NATIONAL GEOGRAPHIC LEARNING | CENGAGE Learning

NATIONAL GEOGRAPHIC LEARNING | CENGAGE Learning

Acknowledgments
Grateful acknowledgment is given to the authors, artists, photographers, museums, publishers, and agents for permission to reprint copyrighted material. Every effort has been made to secure the appropriate permission. If any omissions have been made or if corrections are required, please contact the Publisher.

Cover illustration: Joel Sotelo

Cover Design and Art Direction: Visual Asylum

Illustration Credits: All PM illustrations by National Geographic Learning.

For product information and technology assistance, contact us at
Customer & Sales Support, 888-915-3276

For permission to use material from this text or product, submit all requests online at **www.cengage.com/permissions**
Further permissions questions can be emailed to
permissionrequest@cengage.com

National Geographic Learning | Cengage Learning
1 Lower Ragsdale Drive
Building 1, Suite 200
Monterey, CA 93940

Cengage Learning is a leading provider of customized learning solutions with office locations around the globe, including Singapore, the United Kingdom, Australia, Mexico, Brazil, and Japan. Locate your local office at **www.cengage.com/global**.

Visit National Geographic Learning online at **NGL.Cengage.com**
Visit our corporate website a **www.cengage.com**

ISBN: 978-13054-99027 (Practice Book)

ISBN: 978-13056-58721 (Practice Masters)

Printed in the United States of America
Print Number: 15 Print Year: 2023

Contents

Unit 5: Everything Changes

Unit 6: Better Together

Unit 7: Best Buddies

Unit 8: Our United States

Name ______________________ Date ____________

Phonics

Words with *i, ie, igh*

Circle the word that names the picture.

1.  tie / tea / tail	**2.**  lime / late / light	**3.**  chillled / child / chipped
4.  sigh / say / sea	**5.**  peas / pays / pies	**6.** 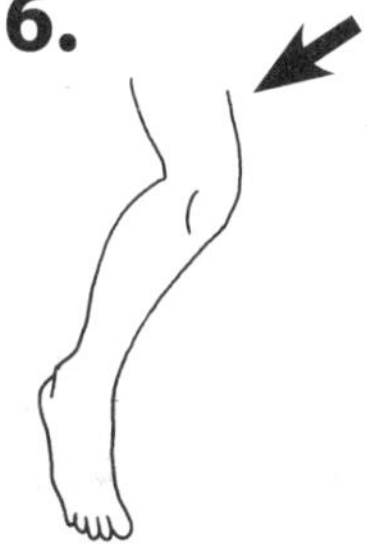 three / thigh / throw
7.  night / neat / nine	**8.** 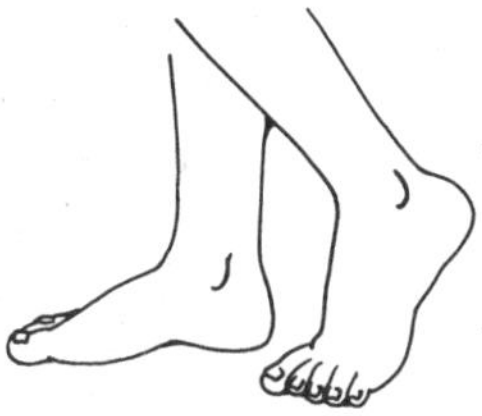 fate / fight / feet	**9.**  crows / cries / cribs
10. 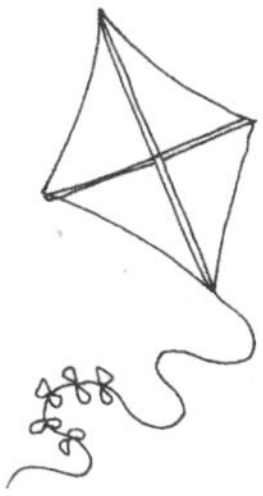 kit / kite / kind	**11.** 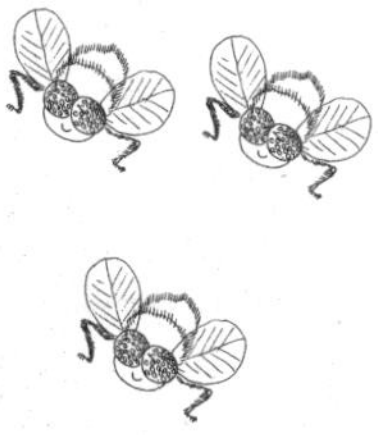 flies / flights / flows	**12.**  leaking / liking / lightning

Read It Together The child flies the kite up high.

Name ______________________ Date ____________

Theme Chart

My Favorite Story

Make a theme chart to tell the details about a favorite story.

Title	Characters
Theme	
Setting	Plot

Work with a partner to find the theme of your story.

Name ______________________ Date __________

Phonics

Words with *i, ie, igh*

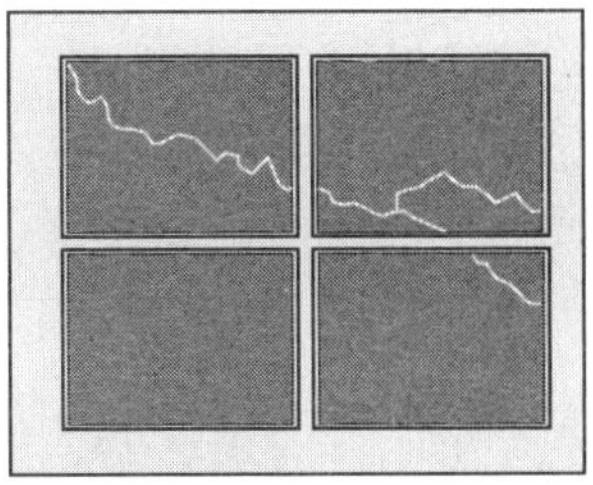

Write the words to complete each sentence.

1. nightlight child

The __________ turns on the __________.

2. lies sighs

He __________ down in bed and __________.

3. right silent

He likes it when the house is as __________ as it is

__________ now!

4. lights night

All of a sudden, something __________ up the __________.

5. upright lightning

Some __________ strikes, and he sits __________.

6. bright fright

It is quite __________, and he is filled with __________.

7. cries find

He __________ out and runs to __________ his mom.

8. delight pie

They eat some __________, and he is filled with __________!

Spelling & Word Work

Word Cards: Words with *i, ie, igh*

 pie	 lightning	 child	 night
flies	find	mild	thigh
nightlight	slight	skies	untied
lies	fright	mind	silent
bright	highway	fight	tie
sigh	vie	iris	necktie
pilot	kind	die	wild

Spelling & Word Work

High Frequency Word Cards

don't	morning
door	air
about	earth
work	hear
should	near
want	even
where	round
important	start
sound	here

Phonics

Words with *kn, gn, wr, mb*

Circle the word that names the picture.

1.

sun
sign
seen

2.

climb
click
cling

3.
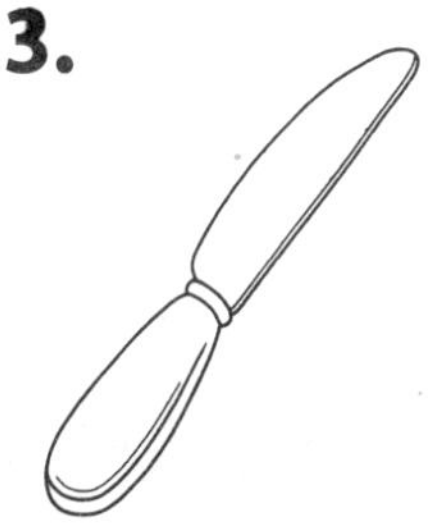

wring
wife
knife

4.

white
write
knight

5.

roam
gnome
comb

6.

kit
knit
quit

7.
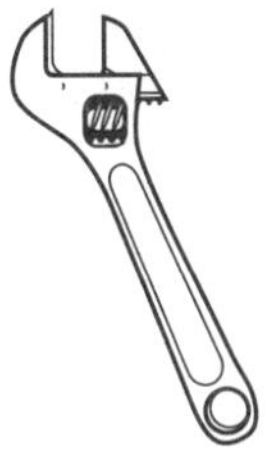

wrench
bench
drench

8.

long
lamb
last

9.
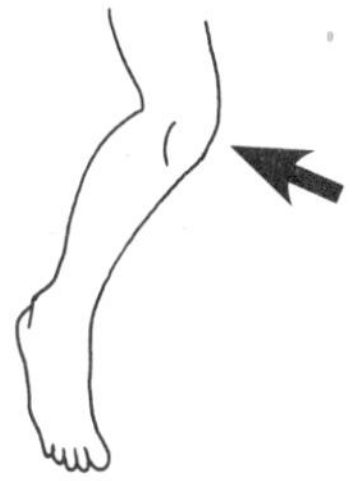

three
know
knee

10.

gnat
wrap
knot

11.

gnash
kneel
wreath

12.
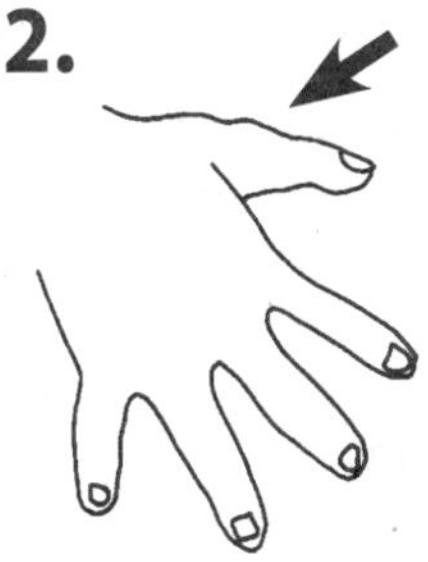

thud
thumb
think

Read It Together Show me your thumb, your wrist, and your knee.

Name ______________________ Date ____________

High Frequency Words

Round and Round

Write a word from the box to complete each sentence.

High Frequency Words
air
earth
even
hear
here
morning
near
round
sound
start

1. They ____________ the ride, and I go round and round.

2. I ____________ the sound of the music playing.

3. I see the ____________ spinning by.

4. I feel the warm morning ____________ blowing on me.

5. Now we are getting ____________ the end of the ride.

6. The ride was ____________ more fun this time than it was before!

7. I think I will come back ____________ to go on this ride one more time.

Name ______________________ Date __________

Grammar: Questions

Use Question Words

Grammar Rules Question Words

Questions that ask for more information often start with *Who, What, Where, Why, When*, or *How*.

Who asks about a person.	*Why* asks for a reason.
What asks about a thing.	*When* asks about a time.
Where asks about a place.	*How* asks how things happen.

Each sentence needs a question word. Spell the question word that belongs with each sentence by filling in the blanks. Work with a partner to see who can complete the word first.

1. __ h __ tells you about weather in your city?
2. W __ __ did it snow early this year?
3. __ __ w does a thermometer work?
4. __ __ e __ will spring begin?
5. W __ __ __ happens when ice melts?
6. __ h __ __ __ is the hottest place on Earth?

Name ______________________ Date ____________

Phonics

Words with *kn, gn, wr, mb*

Write the words to complete each sentence.

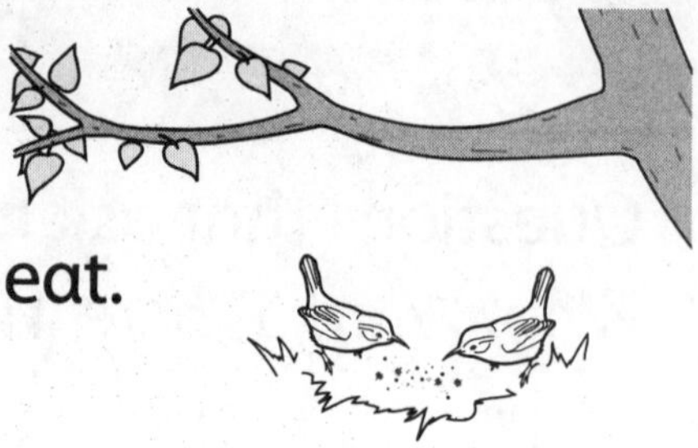

1. **crumbs wrens**

   The ________ might like ________ to eat.

2. **wrap know**

   I ________ how to ________ them in a napkin.

3. **knapsack knot**

   Just tie a ________. Then put them in my ________.

4. **climb lambs**

   We will ________ up this hill and pass those ________.

5. **kneel limb**

   Then we can ________ under a ________ of this tree.

6. **wrists gnats**

   Oh, no! The ________ are starting to bite my ________.

7. **knack wrecking**

   They have a ________ for ________ the day!

8. **wrens crumbs**

   We'll leave the ________ for the ________ to eat and go back home.

Name ______________________ Date ____________

Grammar and Writing

Write Sentences

Read the letter. Then choose an end mark from the box that goes with each sentence. You may use each end mark as many times as you want.

.	?

Hi Grandma,

Thank you very much for the fleece jacket __.__ Can you guess where I am going to wear it ____ Our class is going to the farm next Saturday ____ It might be cold, so I will wear my new fleece jacket ____ Who told you blue was my favorite color ____ I bet it was Dad ____

Love,

Marcie

Name ______________________ Date ____________

Theme Chart

When the Wind Stops

Use clues from the story to figure out the theme.

Title	**Characters**
"When the Wind Stops" makes me think that the story is about nature.	
Setting	**Plot**

Theme

Share your clues and theme with a partner.

Name ______________________ Date ______________

Phonics

Words with *-y*

Circle the word that names the picture.

1.  cry crayon crusty	**2.**  hockey happy hilly	**3.**  know keep key
4.  maybe my money	**5.**  bunny baby by	**6.**  flow fly fluffy
7.  chimney chilly chatty	**8.**  myself mighty muddy	**9.**  pokey pony pry
10.  skinny sigh sky	**11.**  donkey dry dolly	**12.** 50 filthy fry fifty

Read It Together Will you try to ride a pony or a donkey?

Name ______________________ Date ____________

Phonics

Words with *-y*

Write the words to complete each sentence.

1. puppy Billy

_______ puts a leash on his _______.

2. slowly hilly

Then they hike _______ up a _______ path.

3. chilly sky

It is _______ on top, but the _______ is blue and sunny.

4. valley tiny

The people look _______ in the _______ below them.

5. smoky chimneys

Billy sees _______ air coming out of the _______.

6. quickly windy

All of a sudden, it gets very _______, so Billy and his pup run back _______.

7. gusty by

A leaf blows _______ them in the _______ wind. Then another leaf, and another!

8. cozy happy

Billy is _______ to get back to his _______ home!

Name ______________________ Date __________

Phonics

Plurals -s, -es, ies

tail	+	s	=	tails
dish	+	es	=	dishes
bunny – y	+	ies	=	bunnies

Write the word with the correct ending to complete each sentence.

1. dog

I have two ________.

2. baby

One of them had six ________ last month.

3. puppy

All of the ________ are black and white.

4. patch

One is black with white ________ on his body.

5. nose

Two are all white with black ________.

6. tummy

Three are black with white ________.

7. box

All the pups sleep in ________ with blankets inside.

8. family

I will miss them when their ________ pick them up next month.

Spelling & Word Work

Word Cards: Words with *-y*

 jelly	 skyline	 penny	 fly
study	trying	slowly	why
daily	myself	many	why
imaginary	sky	python	fry
heavy	by	sly	very
fancy	January	worry	deny
quickly	dry	carry	type

Spelling & Word Work

High Frequency Word Cards

house	blue
kind	fall
place	also
both	first
been	most
great	family
friend	mountain
different	only
many	every

Name ______________________ Date ____________

Comparison Chart

Compare Author's Purpose

Show why Charlotte Zolotow wrote "When the Wind Stops." Compare this to why Glen Phelan wrote "Day and Night."

Charlotte Zolotow	Glen Phelan
• to tell about how nature changes	• to tell about changes in nature

Tell a partner which selection you liked better. Explain your favorite author's purpose for writing.

Name ______________________ Date ____________

Phonics

Words with Soft *c* and *g*

Sort the words by hard and soft sounds.

cell	gel	candy	gold
cuts	price	badge	spaceship
gallop	changing	flag	picnic

city

1. ______________
2. ______________
3. ______________

cap

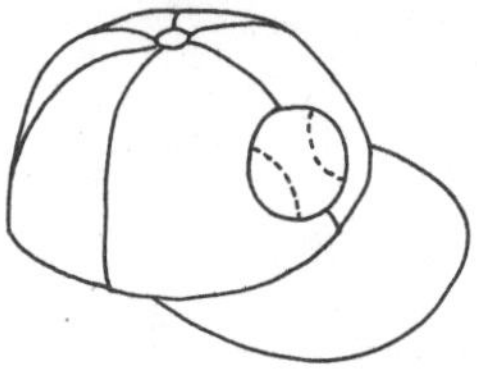

4. ______________
5. ______________
6. ______________

gem

7. ______________
8. ______________
9. ______________

gate

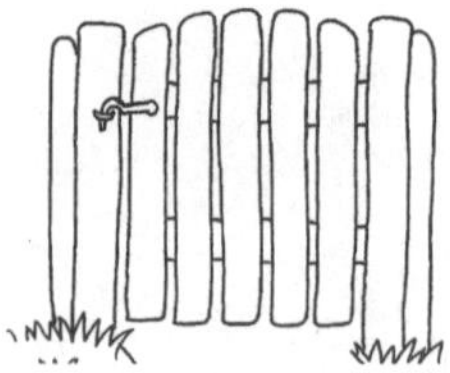

10. ______________
11. ______________
12. ______________

Name ____________________ Date ____________

High Frequency Words

How to Get There

Write a word from the box to complete each sentence.

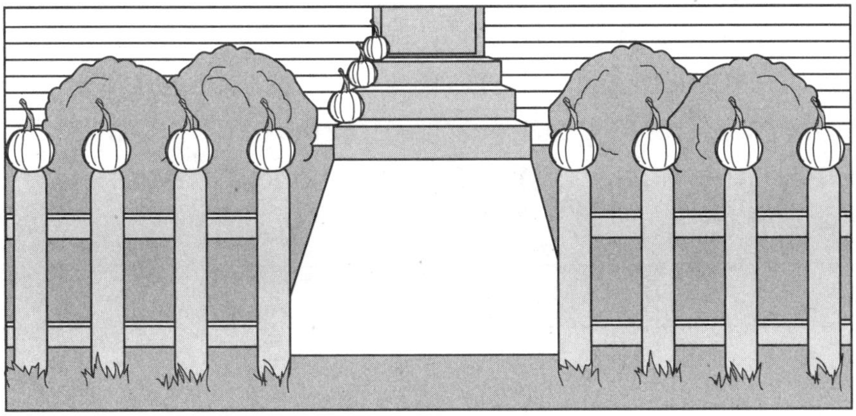

High Frequency Words
also
blue
every
fall
family
first
many
most
mountain
only

Dear Debby,

Here's how to get to my house. First, go past the road to the ________. You will see a bright pink house with a ________ door. It ________ has bright green trim. You can't miss it. There is ________ one house like it! Then go to the right. You will see my house. It's the one with ________ pumpkins on the fence. My ________ puts them there every fall. This fall, we have the ________ pumpkins ever! I can't wait to see you!

Your pal,

Henry

Name ______________________ Date __________

Grammar: Complete Sentences

Mix and Match Sentences

First choose a naming part from column A. Then choose a telling part from column B. Then choose an end mark from column C. Say a sentence using all three parts and any other words you want to add. You may have to change the form of some of the words. After you say your sentence, have your partner tell whether the sentence is a statement, question, command, or exclamation.

A	B	C
I	like	.
Jake	blow	?
Mom	fall	!
our principal	talk	
you	is / are	
the sun	sound	
the rain	feel	
the wind	was / were	
leaves	go	
trees	begin	
it	end	
they	fall	

Name ______________________________ Date ______________

Phonics

Words with Soft *c* and *g*

Write the word that completes each sentence.

1. **city fringe cotton**

   Cindy lives in the ________.

2. **hug huge hedge**

   She can have pets, but they can't be ________.

3. **gems cells mice**

   That's why Cindy has two pet ________.

4. **nice cage badge**

   Her pets live in a screen ________.

5. **space page cent**

   The mice have lots of ________ to hide and to play.

6. **lace judge climb**

   The pets like to ________ up the side of the cage.

7. **smudge judge race**

   They like to ________ around on their wheel.

8. **fancies changes genies**

   Sometimes Cindy ________ the food she gives her pets.

9. **rice range bridge**

   They can eat ________ and oats or food from the pet shop.

Name ______________________________ Date ______________

Grammar and Writing

Write Four Kinds of Sentences

Read the story. Then choose the end mark and letter from the box that tells what kind of sentence each is and write them on the line. You can use each end mark and letter as many times as you want.

.	?	!	
S (Statement)	Q (Questions)	C (Command)	E (Exclamation)

That is the most beautiful tree in the whole world

! E It's right here in our schoolyard ____ Do you know

why the leaves change colors ____ I learned about it

in school ____ Sit down, and I will tell you what I know

____ Stop talking, and listen to me ____

Name ______________________ Date ____________

Grammar: Kinds of Sentences

Build Sentences

1. Play with a partner.
2. Use the words below to build sentences. Write a question, a statement, a command, and an exclamation.
3. Begin with a capital letter. Add an end mark.
4. The player who first writes all four types of sentences correctly wins.

Is / is	night	beautiful
The / the	Do / do	star
Your / your	see	shadow
Come / come	get	you
Are / are	book	That / that

____

____

____

____

____

Name ______________________ Date ____________

Phonics

Words with *oo, ue*

Circle the word that names the picture.

1.  zigzag zee zoo	**2.**  spoon spin Spain	**3.** 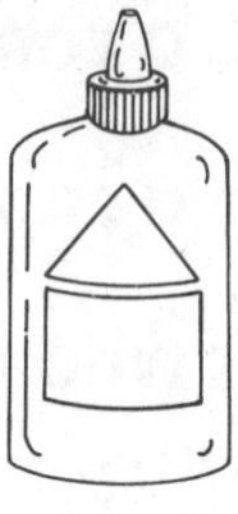 glow glee glue
4.  bloom blow blue	**5.** 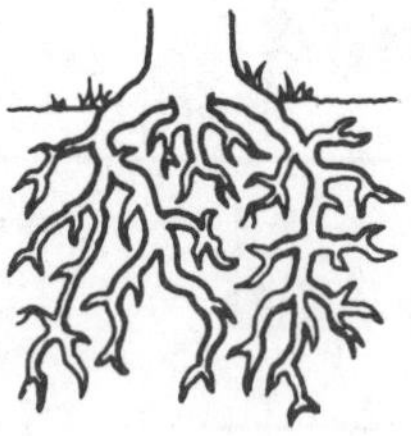 rays roots rows	**6.**  shoot shot shut
7.  bait bat boot	**8.**  try true tray	**9.**  reef roof rude
10.  hoop hop hope	**11.** 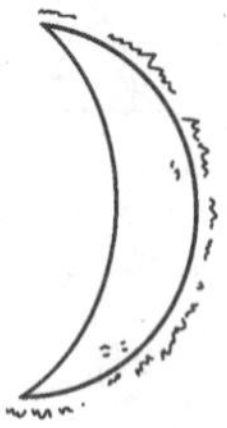 main moon moan	**12.**  die due day

Read It Together Is it true that a shoot has roots and buds?

Name ______________________________ Date ______________

Comparison Chart

Compare and Contrast

Complete the comparison chart below.

Picture Cards	How They Are Alike	How They Are Different
Picture Card 1: ______________		
Picture Card 2: ______________		

Share your chart with a partner. Tell how your picture cards are alike and different.

Name ______________________ Date __________

Phonics

Words with *oo, ue*

Write the word that completes each sentence.

1. **clueless proof moonlight**

   I wake up and see an animal in the ________.

2. **due raccoon room**

   It is a big ________ with a black mask!

3. **snooping true bamboo**

   I think it is ________ around my trash cans to find food.

4. **clues fools moods**

   What are my ________?

5. **roof Tuesday boom**

   I hear a clang and then a ________!

6. **bedroom dues clueless**

   At first I am ________ about what to do.

7. **spoon glued bloom**

   Then I open the window and bang a pan with a ________.

8. **igloo scoot blue**

   While I bang, I yell so that animal will ________.

9. **zooms fondues shampoos**

   It ________ away into the trees. Now I can snooze!

Spelling & Word Work

Word Cards: Words with *oo, ue*

 raccoon	 glue	 pool	 root
balloon	bedroom	avenue	zoom
blue	zoo	igloo	accrue
tooth	moonlight	swoon	duel
fool	proof	true	room
untrue	shampoo	clues	scoot
due	gruel	pursue	unglue

High Frequency Word Cards

may	full
ever	above
nice	far
thank	something
push	goes
around	better
teacher	long
would	talk
while	watch

Name ________________________ Date ______________

Phonics

Endings *-er, -est*

Cut out the cards and mix them up. Sort them by ending. Explain the spelling changes.

fast	**close**
faster	**closer**
fastest	**closest**
sad	**happy**
sadder	**happier**
saddest	**happiest**

Name ____________________ Date ____________

High Frequency Words

What Is It?

Write a word from the box to complete each sentence.

High Frequency Words
above
better
far
full
goes
long
something
talk
watch
while

1. What do I like to ____________ ? I'll give you some clues.

2. It is something far ____________ me up in the sky.

3. I like to ____________ about its phases.

4. When it is full, it shines brightly ____________ I sleep.

5. Two weeks later, the light ____________ away, and I can't see it!

6. It is not out of sight for a ____________ time.

7. That's good, because I like it ____________ when I can see it! What is it?

Name ______________________ Date ____________

Grammar: Yes/No Questions

Use Yes/No Questions

Directions:

1. Make a spinner.
2. Play with a partner.
3. Take turns spinning the spinner.
4. Read the sentence frame. Ask a question using **is, are, does,** or **do.** Then have your partner answer the question with a yes/no answer.

Make a Spinner

1. Put a paper clip over the center of the spinner.
2. Touch the point of a pencil on the middle of the wheel and through the loop of the paper clip.
3. Spin the paper clip to make a spinner.

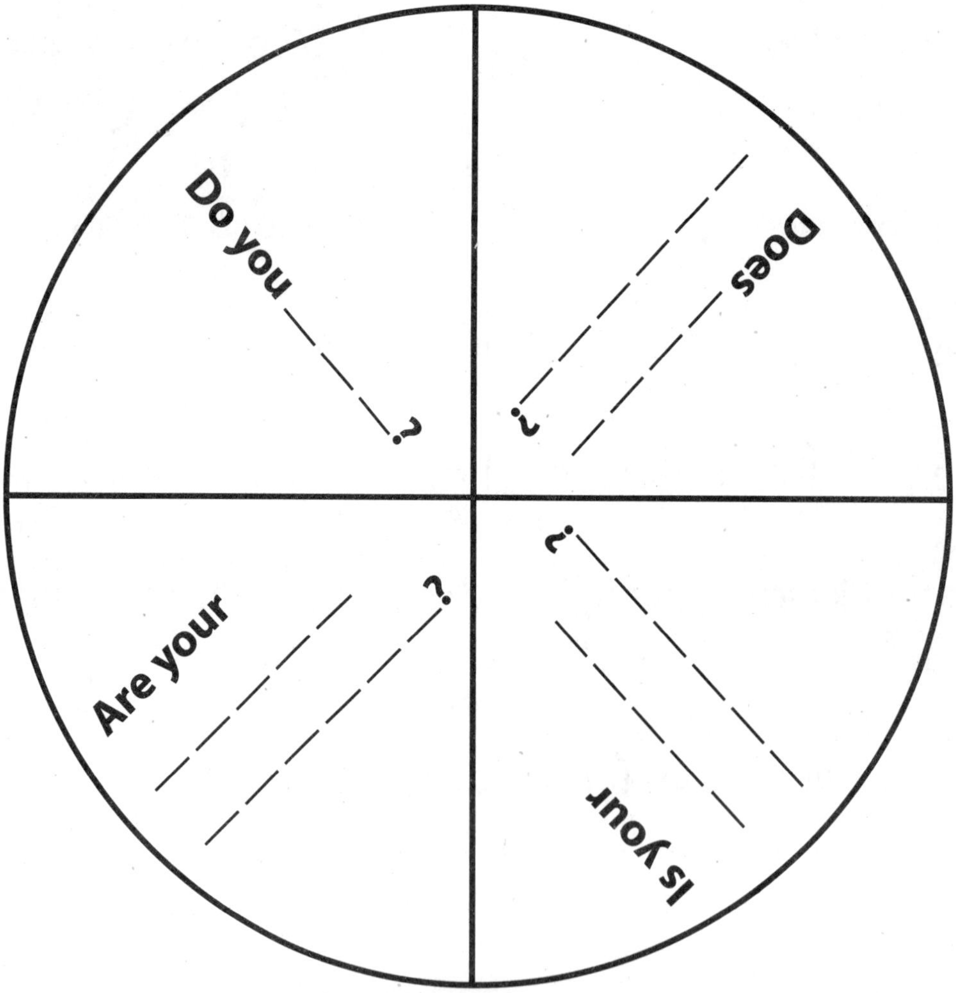

Name ______________________ Date __________

Phonics

Endings *-er*, *-est*

cold			+ er	= colder
brave	– e		+ er	= braver
sad		+ d	+ er	= sadder
lucky	– y	+ i	+ er	= luckier
cold			+ est	= coldest
brave	– e		+ est	= bravest
sad	+ d		+ est	= saddest
lucky	– y	+ i	+ est	= luckiest

Write the word with the correct ending to complete each sentence.

1. close

I live ________ to the beach than Hal.

2. sunny

We pick the ________ days of all to go.

3. hot

Those days can be the ________ days of all, too.

4. tasty

My dad gives us peaches because they are ________ than plums. That's what I think!

5. fast

We have a race to see if Hal swims ________ than I swim.

6. big

Then we jump into the ________ waves.

7. nice

I have a ________ time at the beach with Hal than by myself.

8. happy

We're the ________ of all the kids at the beach!

Name ________________________________ Date ______________

Grammar and Writing

Write Compound Sentences

Read the story. Then choose a word from the box that goes with each sentence. You can use each word as many times as you want.

and	but

My family is going for a walk in the park. I am wearing my light jacket, ___but___ my little brother is wearing his heavy coat. The sun is shining brightly, ________ the wind is chilly. It is early spring, ________ there are some flowers starting to bloom. Winter is gone, ________ we will still have some cold days. Some girls are playing soccer, ________ some boys are watching them. My big sister loves spring, ________ so do I.

Name ______________________ Date __________

Comparison Chart

What Makes the Seasons?

Complete the comparison chart below. Show how the seasons are alike and different.

	Spring	Summer	Fall	Winter
Leaves	sprout			
Raindrops	fall			
Snow	melts			
Days	get longer			

Use the information from the chart to tell your partner how the seasons are alike and different.

Name ______________________________ Date ______________

Phonics

Words with *ue, ew, ui, ou*

Read the sentences and sort the underlined words by sound.

1. <u>Sue</u> sits in the shade under a tree.
2. She is eating <u>fruit</u> when she hears sounds above her.
3. She looks up and sees a <u>few</u> cats stuck in a tree.
4. The cats <u>mew</u> and mew.
5. A <u>group</u> of people comes to help the cats.
6. The crew <u>rescues</u> the cats from the tree.

1. ______________________ 4. ______________________

2. ______________________ 5. ______________________

3. ______________________ 6. ______________________

Name ______________________ Date ____________

Phonics

Words with *ue, ew, ui, ou*

Write the words to complete each sentence.

1. choose foods

What ________ do you ________ to eat?

2. blew soup

Tam has hot ________ for lunch, but she just ________ on it to make it cooler.

3. stew chews

Manny ________ the chunks of meat in his

yummy ________.

4. fruit juice

Kim likes ________ from different kinds of ________.

5. Sue Tuesday

Every ________, my friend ________ eats hot dogs and beans.

6. few cashews

Loc mixes raisins with a ________ kinds of nuts, like

________ and peanuts.

7. fondue new

My family wants to try something ________, so we're

making ________.

Words with *ew, ui, ou, ue*

 jewel	 fruit	 cruise	 soup
cue	fewer	rescue	you
crew	continue	virtue	wound
bruised	hue	nephew	chew
argue	pewter	grew	group
new	rouge	screw-driver	blew
juice	knew	value	statue

Spelling & Word Work

High Frequency Word Cards

yes	again
say	between
write	almost
dear	never
name	went
letter	any
says	below
answer	grow
tomorrow	surprise

Name ____________ Date ____________

Venn Diagram

Compare Genres

Use the Venn diagram to tell how "What Makes the Seasons?" and "A Winter Wonder" are alike and different.

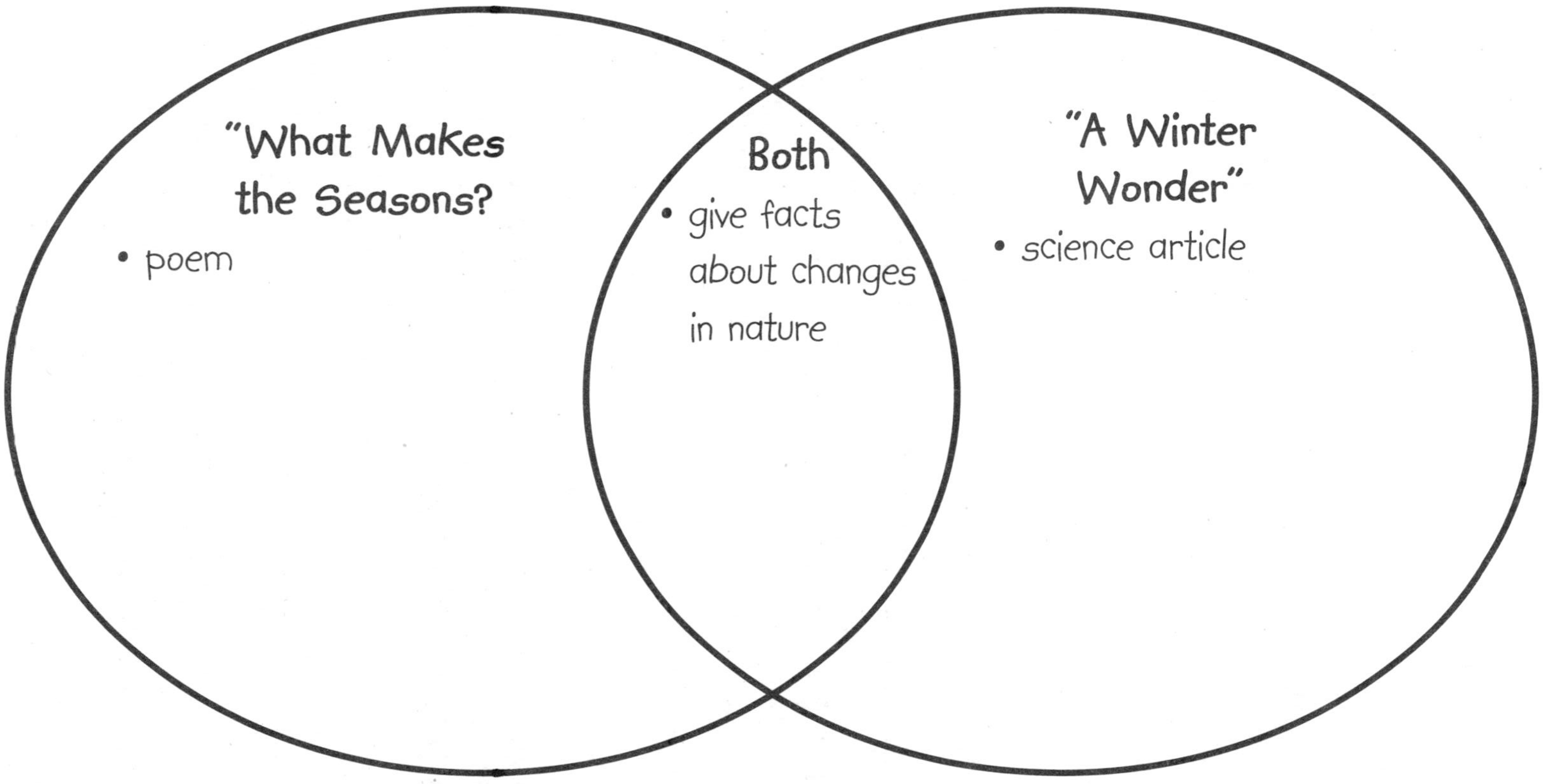

Tell a partner one way the selections are the same and one way they are different.

Name ________________________________ Date ______________

Phonics

Endings *-s, -es, -ed, -ing*

Write the word that completes each sentence.

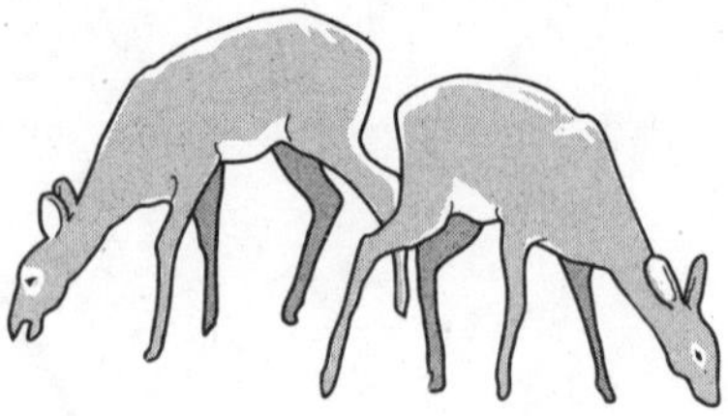

1. likes planning

Ralph ________ animals.

2. chewed studies

He ________ them when he is outside.

3. hiked flies

Last week, Ralph ________ near the mountains.

4. spotted growing

He ________ some deer and a moose.

5. smiling tried

He ________ to take some photos, but the animals ran away.

6. fixed jogging

Now Ralph is ________ at the beach.

7. hopping hoping

He is ________ to see some seagulls.

8. bloomed catches

He does see one! It swoops down and ________ a fish!

9. carrying snooped

Now it is ________ its food away.

Name ______________________ Date ____________

High Frequency Words

Surprises

Write a word from the box to complete each sentence.

High Frequency **Words**
again
almost
any
below
between
grow
never
surprise
tomorrow
went

Mom had a ________ for me last weekend. I went to my swim class and came back ________ 2:00 and 2:30. I never expected to see ________ friends at my house. That's why I ________ jumped a mile high when all my friends yelled, "Surprise!" We hit a homemade donkey once, and then we hit it ________. It broke, and treats fell onto the grass ________. Now I have a surprise for Mom. Tomorrow we will plant a tree. Then we will watch it ________.

Name ______________________________ Date ______________

Grammar: Questions

Match Sentences

First read a statement in column A. Then find the question in column B that is made from that statement. Draw a line from the statement to the question. Take turns with a partner.

A	B
That is your hat.	Is it raining outside?
I am in the second grade.	Is she my aunt?
We are best friends.	Are they big and strong?
It is raining outside.	Is he late for school?
She is my aunt.	Am I on your team?
I am a soccer player.	Are we best friends?
They are big and strong.	Is that your hat?
I am on your team.	Are you funny?
He is late for school.	Am I in the second grade?
You are funny.	Am I a soccer player?

Name ________________________ Date ____________

Phonics

Endings *-s, -es, -ed, -ing*

Write the word with the correct ending that completes each sentence.

hum	+ s	= hums	like	+ s	= likes	cry – y + i + es	= cries
hum + m	+ ed	= hummed	like – e + ed	= liked		cry – y + i + ed	= cried
hum + m	+ ing	= humming	like – e + ing	= liking		cry	+ ing	= crying

1. **bake**

   Last week, Dad and I ________ a pecan pie.

2. **plan**

   We were ________ to bring it to Grandma.

3. **try**

   The pie smelled so good that we ________ a bite.

4. **taste**

   Soon my mom was ________ it, too.

5. **stop**

   By the time we ________ eating, there was no pie left!

6. **make**

   Now we are ________ Grandma a cake.

7. **dry**

   I wash dishes and Dad ________ them, while the cake bakes.

8. **write**

   Mom ________ a sign for the cake. It says, "No eating!"

Name ______________________________ Date ______________

Grammar and Writing

Write Questions

Read the letter. Then choose a word from the box that goes with each sentence.

Who	What	When	Where	Why	How

Dear Richard,

How are you and your family? Everyone here is fine. I have a lot of questions about your trip to Mexico. ________ did you get back from your trip? Was the weather nice? ________ did you stay? Did you stay in a hotel or in a condo? ________ was your favorite activity? I bet it was snorkeling. You wrote me a postcard from Mexico. ________ did you choose a postcard with a palm tree on it? You made me want to go on a trip, too! ________ took care of your dog and birds while you were gone? Write back as soon as you can.

Your friend,

Ramesh

Name ________________________ Date ____________

Grammar: Questions

Use Punctuation

Grammar Rules **Questions**

- A question ends with a question mark. (?)
- The answer to a question ends with a period. (.)

Add correct punctuation to each of the sentences.

1. Who likes winter as much as I do

2. Many people think winter is a great season

3. Is it because there are fun things to do in the snow

4. Yes, I think it is

5. What are your favorite winter activities

6. I like to sled, ski, and build forts in the snow

7. Do you ever get cold in winter

8. No, I do not get cold because I dress warmly

Name ______________________ Date ____________

Phonics

Words with *ar*

Use paper fasteners and paper clips to make two spinners. Spin them both and use the letters to make words below. If the letters don't make a word, spin again.

Make Spinners

1. Push a brad through the center of the spinner.
2. Open the brad on the back.
3. Hook a paper clip over the brad on the front to make a spinner.

Beginning of word

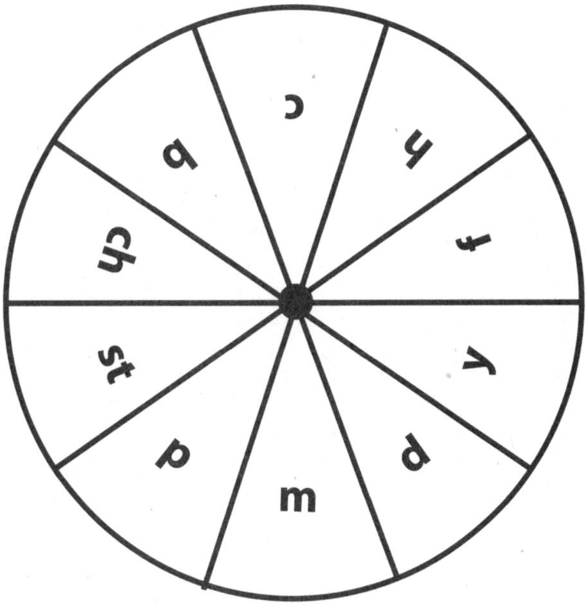

End of word

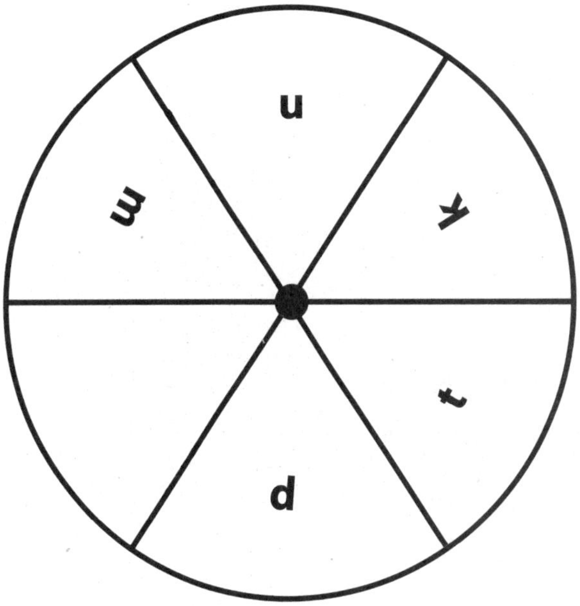

1. car ____________
2. ar ____________
3. ar ____________
4. ar ____________
5. bark ____________
6. ar ____________
7. ar ____________
8. ar ____________
9. ar ____________
10. ar ____________
11. ar ____________
12. ar ____________

Name ______________________ Date ____________

Story Map

Story Elements

Use a story map to tell about the characters, setting, and plot of a story.

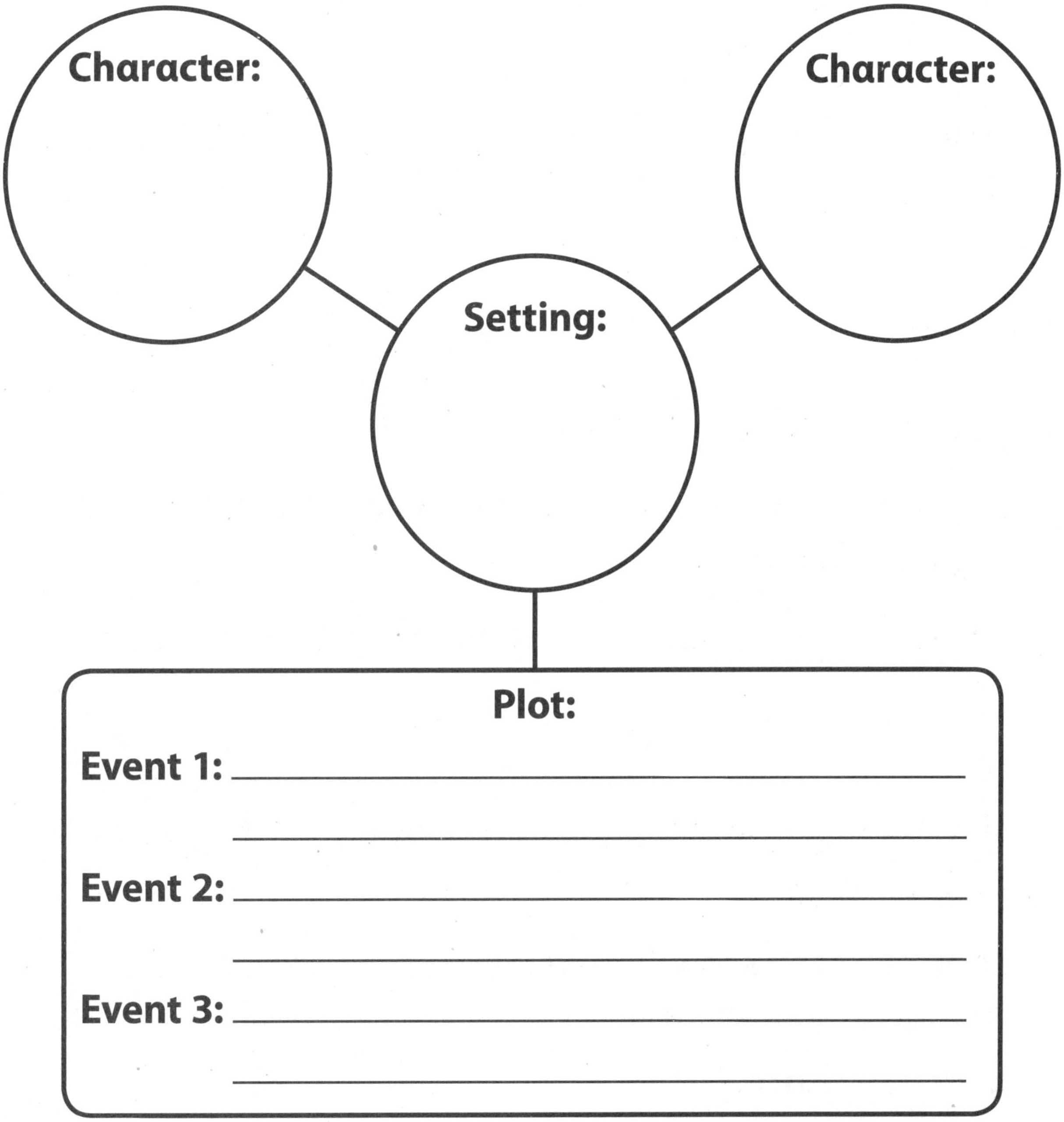

Use your story map to tell a partner a story about being part of a team.

Name ______________________ Date ____________

Phonics

Words with *ar*

Write the words to complete each sentence.

1. **yard shark**

   Look outside. Would you see a ______ in the ______?

2. **car parked**

   No! You might see a ______ that is ______ in the driveway!

3. **Mars farm**

   Visit a local ______. Would you see the planet ______ there?

4. **barn large**

   No! You might see ______ bales of hay inside the ______.

5. **dark start**

   Look up at the ______ sky at midnight. Would you see the sun ______ to shine?

6. **far stars**

   No! You might see ______ that are very ______ away.

7. **smart march**

   Look at all the snow. Would it be ______ to ______ outside in your swimsuit?

8. **charge scarf**

   No! You might put on your jacket, ______, hat, boots, and mittens and then ______ outside to play in the snow!

Word Cards: Words with *ar*

 charm	 farm	 car	 jar
charge	dart	march	far
harp	bar	jar	fort
mar	par	hate	tar
chart	purrs	art	card
for	part	tart	tarp
tore	hard	lard	north

Spelling & Word Work

High Frequency Word Cards

here	get
near	buy
morning	old
air	just
earth	school
hear	children
sound	found
start	began
round	another
even	together

Name ______________________ Date ____________

Phonics

Longer Words with *ar*

Circle the word that names the picture.

1.

garnish
gumdrop
garden

2.

artist
army
attic

3.

mattress
market
marshland

4.

stoplight
starfish
sandwich

5.
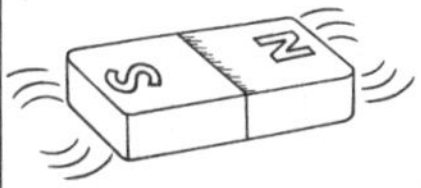
magnet
margin
mammal

6.
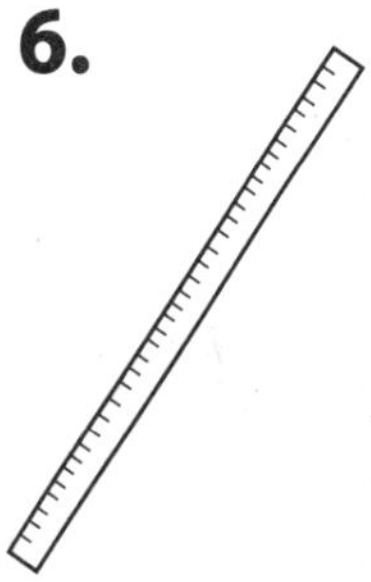
yippee
yellow
yardstick

7.
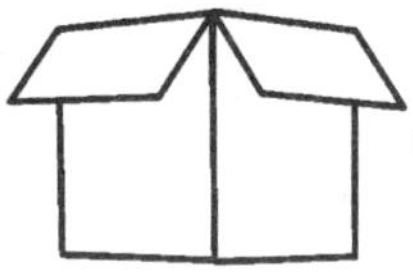
catnap
carpet
carton

8.

partner
party
parking

9.

cartoon
classroom
charcoal

10.

garlic
gateway
gallop

11.

parsley
partway
postmark

12.

boxcar
barking
button

Read It Together The artist has a party in her garden.

Name ______________________ Date ____________

High Frequency Words

Lost and Found

Write a word from the box to complete each sentence.

High Frequency Words
another
began
buy
children
found
get
just
old
school
together

Mark and Lars were walking home from school ________. They ________ a lost dog. The dog was not old. It was ________ a puppy. The dog ________ to follow them home. The children saw one sign and then ________ one. The signs said "Lost Puppy."

"When we ________ home, Mom can call these people on the phone," Mark said.

"Maybe Mom can ________ us a puppy to keep!" Lars exclaimed.

Name ______________________________ Date ____________

Grammar: Subject and Object Pronouns

Mix and Match Sentences

Read a sentence in column A. Then draw a line to a word in column B that can replace the underlined part of the sentence. Have your partner say the sentence using the word from column B. Take turns drawing a line and saying the sentence. You can use the words in column B more than once.

A	B
Mr. Adams cuts the grass.	he
Give the shovel to the girl.	
Mrs. Adams is a good gardener.	she
That tree is huge!	
Walk to the garden with your sister.	it
Is David raking the leaves now?	
Help Mr. Adams with that heavy bag.	we
Do your parents like gardening?	
Give the bag to the boys.	they
Gardening is fun for my brother.	
Aunt June and I will plant some seeds.	him
Hand this watering can to Aunt June.	
Don't stand under that tree in a lightning storm.	her

Name ______________________________ Date ______________

Phonics

Longer Words with *ar*

Write the word that completes each sentence.

1. **arctic cartoons postmarks**

   Sometimes on weekends, Tess watches __________ on TV.

2. **barnyard yardstick charcoal**

   One of them is about pigs in a __________.

3. **scarlet armhole harvest**

   Once, the pigs got into the farm's __________.

4. **margin backyard parsley**

   They ate all the parsnips and __________!

5. **farmhand starlight carpet**

   A __________ had to chase the pigs away.

6. **barbell partway army**

   When he was __________ across the yard, he slipped and fell in some mud. He could not get up.

7. **hardship cargo farmer**

   The __________ came to help him, but it was hard and he slipped, too.

8. **party market artist**

   The pigs watched and squealed. Did they think it was a funny mud __________? The farmers thought it was funny. Tess did, too.

Name ______________________________ Date ______________

Grammar and Writing

Write Pronouns

Read the story. Then choose the word from the box that correctly replaces the underlined word or words in each sentence.

I	he	him	her	it	we

Dad and I like to bake things. Dad and I We are making bread today. I hand Dad ________ the flour from the cupboard. He mixes the flour ________ with water, salt, and yeast. Dad says, "This bread will taste great to Mom, you, and me ________, won't it?" Then Dad ________ kneads the bread for ten minutes. Dad pops the bread into the oven. Dad says, "Dad ________ didn't tell Mom we would be baking today." "I want to surprise Mom ________."

Name ______________________________ Date ______________

Story Map

Domino Soup

Make a story map for "Domino Soup."

Character:
Abuelo

Character

Character:

Setting:
Little Havana
in Miami

Plot:

Event 1: Abuelo wins at dominoes.

Event 2: ______________________________

Event 3: ______________________________

Event 4: ______________________________

Share your story map with a partner. Compare the story elements you found for "Domino Soup."

Name ______________________ Date ____________

Phonics

Words with *or, ore*

Unscramble each word and write it. Then write a sentence using the word.

1. o h n r h o r n I play the horn in a band.	**2. e t o r** ___ ___ ___ ___
3. c n r o ___ ___ ___ ___	**4. r f o t** ___ ___ ___ ___
5. h r c e o ___ ___ ___ ___ ___	**6. r s o h t** ___ ___ ___ ___ ___
7. e n s r o ___ ___ ___ ___ ___	**8. o c r h p** ___ ___ ___ ___ ___

Name ______________________ Date ____________

Phonics

Words with *or, ore*

Write the words to complete each sentence.

1. chores Mort

What does _______ do when he finishes his _______?

2. porch sports

He sits on his _______ and watches a _______ game on TV.

3. more score

He is hoping that his team will _______ some _______ runs.

4. horse snort

Then he hears a _______ from his _______ in the barn.

5. north storm

He looks up and sees a big _______ coming from the _______.

6. store torch

He runs to the _______ to buy a _______ and some other supplies.

7. forth shore

He sees sand whipping back and _______ by the _______.

8. force before

Mort is glad to be safely at home _______ the full _______ of the storm hits!

Spelling & Word Work

Word Cards: Words with *or, ore*

 horse	 chore	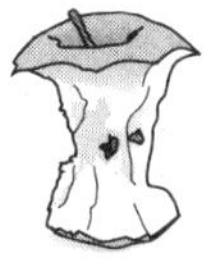 core	 shore
sports	tore	sore	or
bore	force	stork	more
wore	corn	for	yore
nor	pork	snore	port
sort	spore	torn	ore
store	porch	born	score

Spelling & Word Work

High Frequency Word Cards

family	line
mountain	done
every	side
blue	try
only	once
first	must
fall	next
many	funny
most	follow
also	laugh

Name ____________________ Date ____________

Comparison Chart

Compare Two Versions of the Same Story

Use the comparison chart to show how "Domino Soup" and "Stone Soup" are alike and different.

	"Domino Soup"	"Stone Soup"
Type of Story	play	song
Characters		
Setting		
Plot		

Tell a partner how the two versions of the story are the same and different.

Name ______________________ Date __________

Phonics

Longer Words with *or, ore*

Circle the word that names the picture.

1.  porthole proceed provide	**2.**  thanking tardy thorny	**3.** 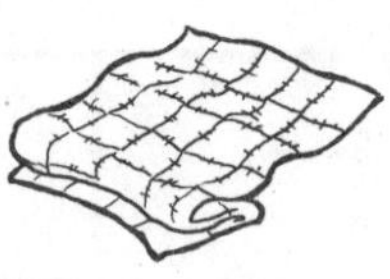 before blanket boring
4.  forecast forest fastest	**5.**  acorn accuse adore	**6.**  porridge porthole popcorn
7.  motor market morning	**8.**  carport corncob cactus	**9.**  horseback hornet harness
10. **40** forty forgive favor	**11.**  odor organ orphan	**12.**  snowstorm snorkel snoring

Read It Together We saw acorns and hornets in the forest this morning.

Name ______________________ Date ______________

High Frequency Words

This Way or That Way?

Write a word from the box to complete each sentence.

High Frequency Words
done
follow
funny
laugh
line
must
next
once
side
try

1. I am in a ________ play at school.
2. I stand at the end of a long ________ of actors.
3. I ________ follow them and do what they do.
4. They all run to one ________ of the stage, but I run the other way.
5. That makes all the people ________ really hard!
6. I try again, but the ________ time they run left, and I run right!
7. Once the play is ________, the people say that they laughed at me the most.

Name ______________________ Date ____________

Grammar: Subject and Object Pronouns

Use Subject and Object Pronouns

Directions:

1. Make a spinner.
2. Play with a partner.
3. Take turns spinning the spinner.
4. Say a sentence using one of the words you landed on. Then have your partner say a sentence using the other word you landed on.

Make a Spinner

1. Put a paper clip in the center of the circle.
2. Hold one end of the paper clip with a pencil.
3. Spin the paper clip around the pencil.

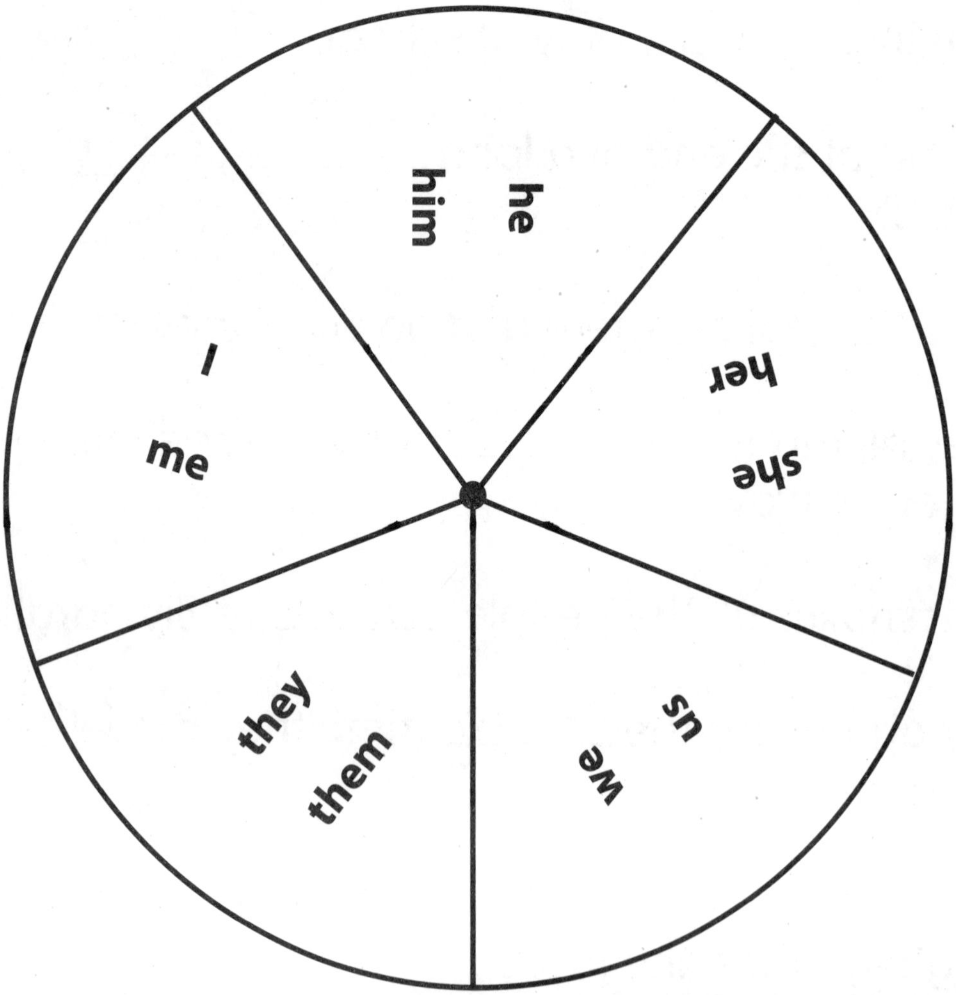

Name ______________________________ Date ______________

Phonics

Longer Words with *or, ore*

Write the word that completes each sentence.

1. **seashore hornet effort**

   Tory is at the ________ with her family.

2. **pitchfork porridge explore**

   She wants to ________ the beach and look for fish in the water.

3. **export forecast favor**

   She wakes up in the morning, but the ________ is for rain.

4. **northwest stormy morning**

   It might get too ________ to be on the beach!

5. **forest ignore boring**

   What will Tory do? It is ________ to stay inside the cabin!

6. **popcorn thorny adore**

   "I know!" says Dad. "We can play games and eat ________."

7. **forgets before orphan**

   Tory has so much fun that she ________ all about the rainstorm.

8. **corncob odor report**

   The next morning, the ________ is for a hot, sunny day.

9. **snorkel organ porthole**

   Tory goes to the beach with her ________. Which fish will she see?

Name ______________________________ Date ______________

Grammar and Writing

Write Subject and Object Pronouns

Read the story. Then choose the word from the box that correctly completes each sentence.

me	her	she	them	they	us

I love my grandmother. Having Grandma over for supper is a lot of fun for __me__. Grandma looked hungry when ________ sat down at the table. Mom, Dad, and I all smiled at her, and she smiled back at ________. I said, "We picked the tomatoes for the soup in our garden. ________ were really red and ripe." Grandma answered, "Yes, I know. I saw ________ sitting on the windowsill this afternoon." Mom asked Grandma to pass the muffins to ________. We had a great meal.

Name ____________________ Date __________

Grammar: Pronouns

Use Pronouns

Make a Spinner

1. Put a paper clip in the center of the circle.
2. Hold one end of the paper clip with a pencil.
3. Spin the paper clip around the pencil.

Directions:

1. Play with a partner.
2. Spin the spinner.
3. Name a pronoun to replace the words in the space.
4. Say a sentence using the pronoun.
5. Color in the space.
6. Play until all the spaces are colored in.

Phonics

Words with *er, ir, ur*

Cut out the words and mix them up. Then sort them by *er*, *ir*, and *ur* spellings.

fern	first
her	third
herd	burn
perch	burst
birch	church
bird	fur

Name ______________________ Date ____________

Main Idea Diagram

Main Idea

Make a main idea diagram to tell about a time you worked with someone to reach a goal.

Detail

Detail

Main Idea

Share your main idea diagram with a partner.

Name ______________________________ Date ______________

Phonics

Words with *er, ir, ur*

Write the words on the line to complete each sentence.

1. **hers urges**

   Gert ________ a friend of ________ to hike in the forest.

2. **Kurt serves**

   "The forest ________ as a home to a lot of wildlife," she tells ________.

3. **first bird**

   The ________ thing they see is a ________.

4. **perch chirps**

   It ________ from its ________ on the branch of a tree.

5. **fern curled**

   Then they see a snake ________ around a green ________.

6. **third fur**

   The ________ thing they see is a fox with red ________.

7. **fir turns**

   It stands at the edge of a small field and then ________ and trots between two ________ trees.

8. **curve birch**

   The pals walk around a ________ in the path and pass a white ________ tree as they walk out of the forest.

Spelling & Word Work

Word Cards: Words with *er, ir, ur*

 shirt	 bird	 mother	 curl
squirm	serve	third	herd
fir	term	girl	dirt
nerve	her	flirt	after
father	birth	burn	nurse
fur	sir	hurt	surf
turn	sister	squirt	spurt

Spelling & Word Work

High Frequency Word Cards

watch	boy
while	us
goes	pull
above	gave
talk	took
long	myself
far	upon
something	brother
better	sister
full	always

Name ____________________ Date ____________

Phonics

Longer Words with *er, ir, ur*

Circle the word that names the picture.

1.  ruler rubber river	**2.**  squirting summer squirrel	**3.** 13 thirteen thirsty Thursday
4.  tiger turkey termite	**5.**  spider spurted survive	**6.**  city sister circus
7.  teacher turnip thirty	**8.**  burger bigger birthday	**9.**  gerbil giraffe gopher
10.  lurching letter lobster	**11.**  perfume paper perfect	**12.**  farmer furry firsthand

Read It Together Are turkeys, spiders, lobsters, or squirrels furry?

Name ______________________ Date ______________

High Frequency Words

Tugging Rope

Write a word from the box to complete each sentence.

High Frequency Words
always
boy
brother
gave
myself
pull
sister
took
upon
us

1. "I want to play a game," said the boy, "but I can't play by ________."

2. "I'll ask my brother, my ________, and my friends."

3. One team ________ one end of a rope, and one team grabbed the other end.

4. All the kids started to ________ hard.

5. One team ________ a really hard tug!

6. All the kids fell ________ the grass!

7. "We always fall when you tug hard," exclaimed the boy, "but you always fall with ________!"

Name ______________________ Date __________

Grammar: Possessive Pronouns

Use Possessive Pronouns

Directions:

1. Make a spinner.
2. Play with a partner.
3. Take turns spinning the spinner.
4. Read the word. Say a sentence using the possessive pronoun you landed on. Then have your partner say another sentence using the same possessive pronoun.

Make a Spinner

1. Put a paper clip  in the center of the circle.
2. Hold one end of the paper clip with a pencil.
3. Spin the paper clip around the pencil.

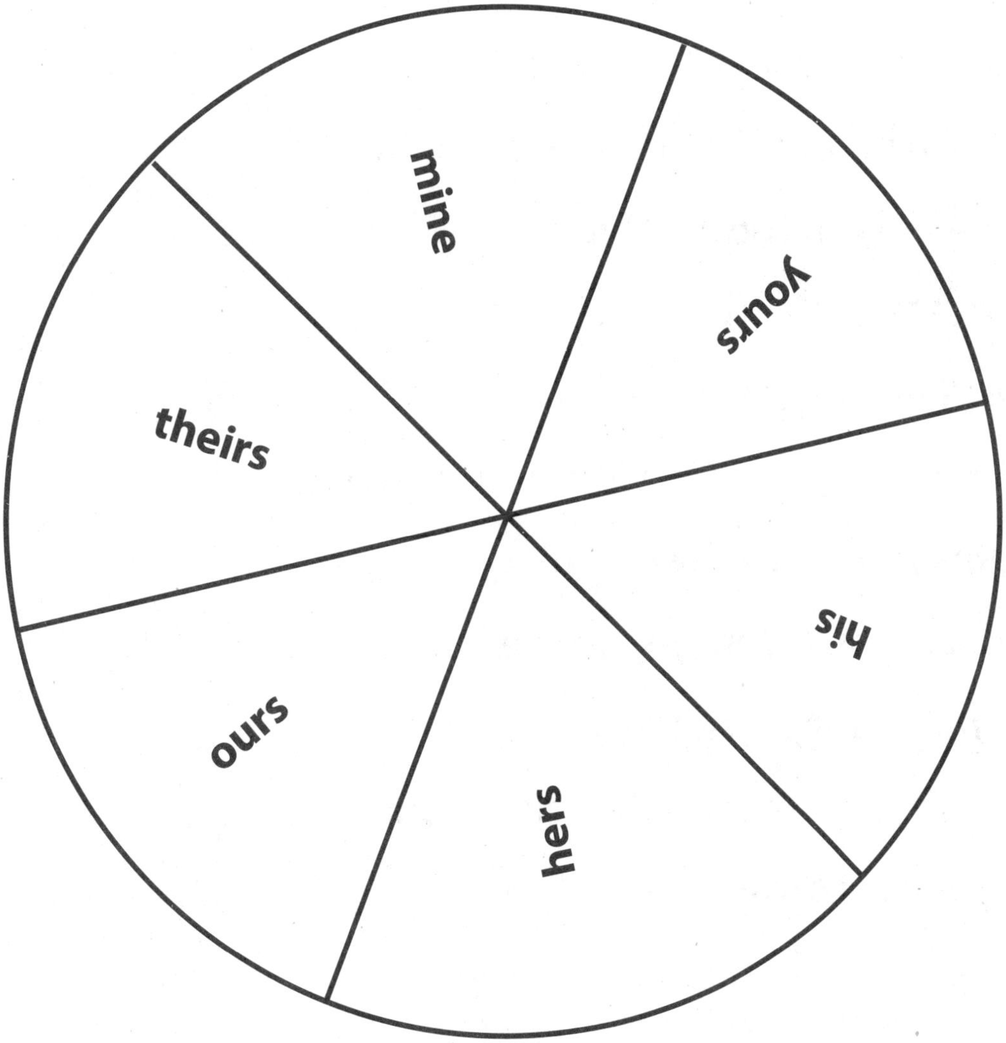

Name ______________________ Date ____________

Phonics

Longer Words with *er, ir, ur*

Write the word that completes each sentence.

1. **crater blurry perfect**

   Shirley thinks that her two pet gerbils are ________ pets.

2. **birthday ladder murmur**

   They were a ________ gift from her mom and dad.

3. **surprised winter person**

   Shirley was ________ and happy when she got them!

4. **painter desert herself**

   She found out that gerbils come from the ________.

5. **after Thursday thirsty**

   That's why they don't get too ________.

6. **survive blurry sternly**

   They can ________ without a lot of water!

7. **hamsters numbers dirty**

   Some people confuse gerbils and ________.

8. **furry thirty perform**

   Gerbils are the ones that have long, ________ tails.

9. **pepper turnip chirping**

   When they are happy, they make ________ sounds.

Name ______________________ Date __________

Grammar and Writing

Write Possessive Pronouns

Read the letter. Then choose the word from the box that correctly completes each sentence.

mine	yours	his	hers	ours	theirs

Hello.

My name is Pencho Ragbey and I live in Tibet. I want to tell you about a special project of ___ours___. Our life in Tibet is very different from ________ in the United States. Here, many children do not go to school. ________ is a hard life of farming and herding.

But this is changing. We worked together to build a school for our village. My sister Tsering helped start a group. The idea for the group was ________. One of my teachers helps us learn to use a computer. The first computer at school was ________, but now we have others. I am writing to you on a new computer. This one is ________!

Sincerely,
Pencho Ragbey

Name ______________________ Date ____________

Apply Word Knowledge

Vocabulary Bingo

1. Write one Key Word in each school.
2. Listen to the clues. Find the Key Word and color it in.
3. Say "Bingo" when you have four markers in a row.

Key Words	
dream	plan
education	project
join	result
opportunity	skills
organize	success

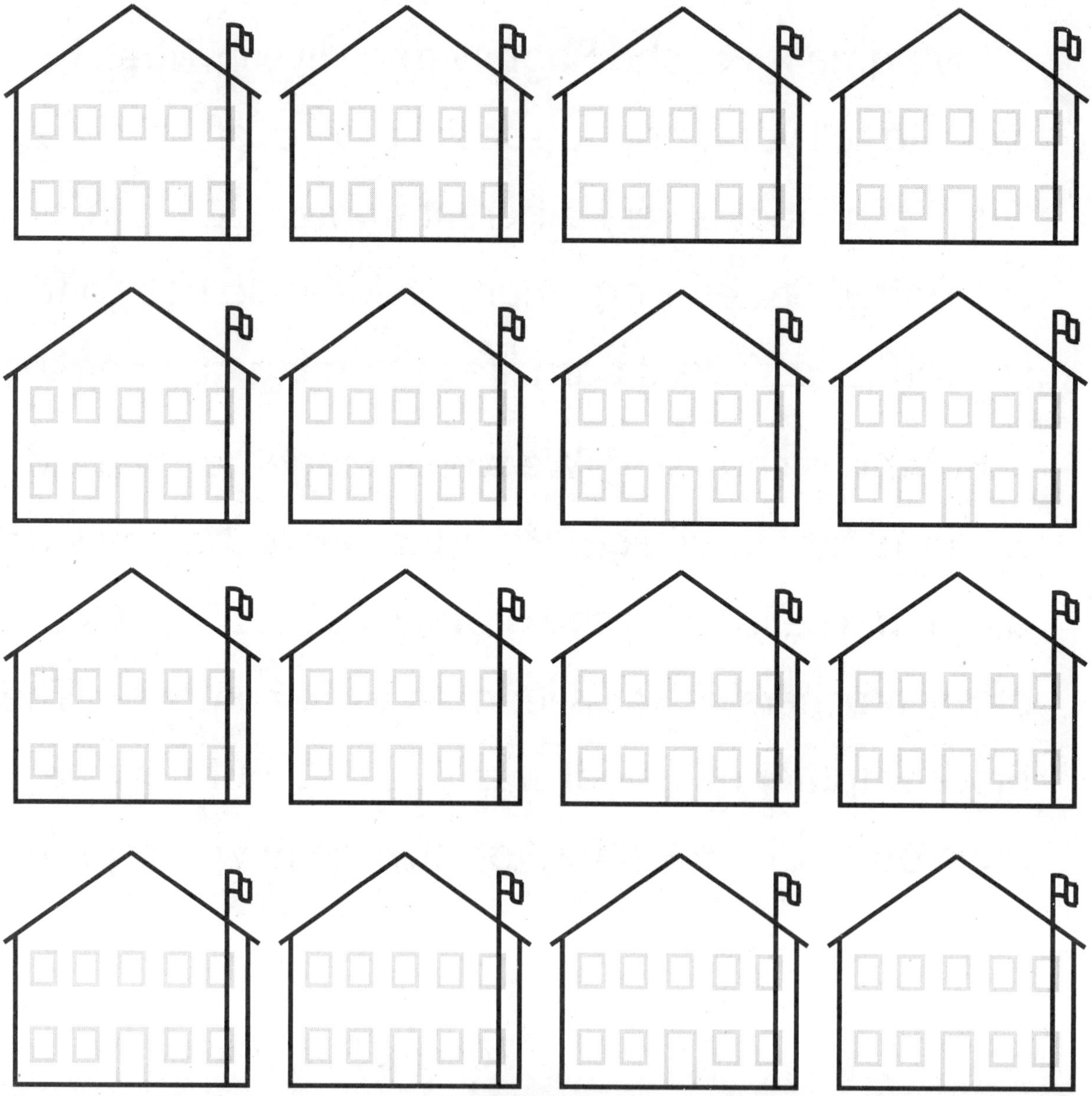

Name ______________________ Date ____________

Main Idea Diagram

In a Mountain Community

Make a main idea diagram for "In a Mountain Community."

Detail	Detail
The people of Chungba raise money for a school.	

Main Idea

Share your main idea diagram with a partner. See if you found the same main idea.

Name ______________________________ Date ______________

Phonics

Words with *air, are, ear*

Circle the word that names the picture.

1.  bake bear blare	**2.**  squeak squirt square	**3.**  sharp share shore
4.  peer pore pear	**5.** 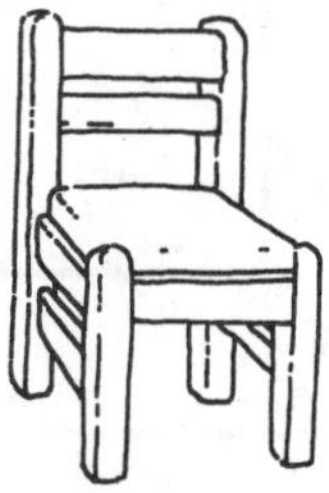 chase chair chain	**6.** 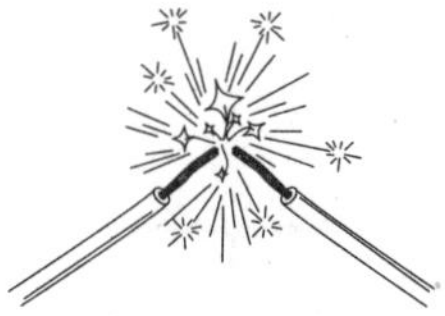 spread spare spark
7. 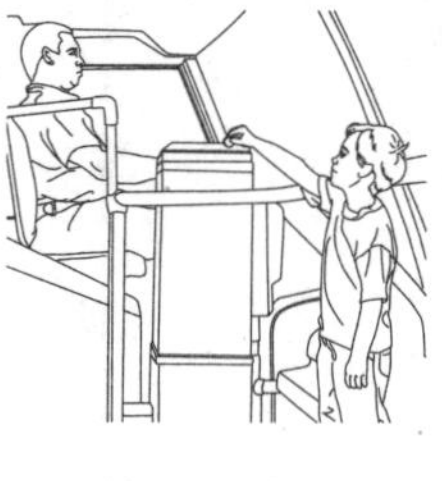 fare far frame	**8.**  hard hare hurt	**9.**  pay peak pair
10.  pare park part	**11.**  air aim awake	**12.**  hair hear her

Read It Together We saw a pair of hares share some grass.

Name ______________________ Date ____________

Phonics

Words with *air, are, ear*

Write the words to complete each sentence.

1. **chair airplane**

   Vic falls asleep in his __________ on the __________.

2. **scary nightmare**

   He has a __________ that is __________.

3. **hair stare**

   First, people __________ at him because his __________ is green.

4. **pear mare**

   Next, a hungry __________ chases him because she wants to eat his __________.

5. **scare bear**

   Then he gets an even bigger __________ when a furry __________ chases him up a tree!

6. **hares fair**

   Then, he is at a __________ and sees two huge __________.

7. **pair rare**

   It is a __________ sight to see the __________ chasing him!

8. **staircase daring**

   Vic makes a __________ escape up a __________.

Spelling & Word Work

Word Cards: Words with *air, are, ear*

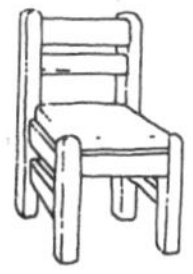 chair	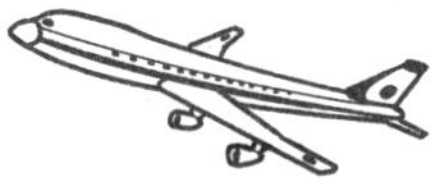 airplane	 hare	 bear
stair	lair	mare	hairy
share	care	rare	glare
pear	hair	stare	pair
air	wear	fairy	bare
fair	scare	dare	dairy
tear	spare	swear	fare

Spelling & Word Work

High Frequency Word Cards

almost	made
again	five
tomorrow	four
between	men
went	night
surprise	such
never	well
any	wish
grow	second
below	thought

Name ______________________ Date ____________

Comparison Chart

Compare Texts

Use the comparison chart to show how "In a Mountain Community" and "Mi Barrio" are alike and different.

	"In a Mountain Community"	**"Mi Barrio"**
It is in an urban community.		✓
It is in a rural community.	✓	
The community members help each other.		
The children help their community, too.		
The selection is illustrated with photographs.		
It is a true story.		

Compare your chart with a partner's. See if you found the same information.

Name ______________________ Date ____________

Phonics

Words with *eer, ear*

Circle the word that names the picture.

1.  deer, dare, deeper	**2.** 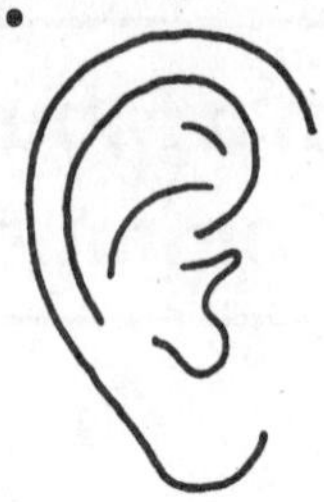 air, ore, ear	**3.**  tire, tear, tore
4.  spear, speak, seal	**5.**  hair, hear, heat	**6.**  store, street, steer
7.  beard, bored, bird	**8.**  fear, farm, fair	**9.** 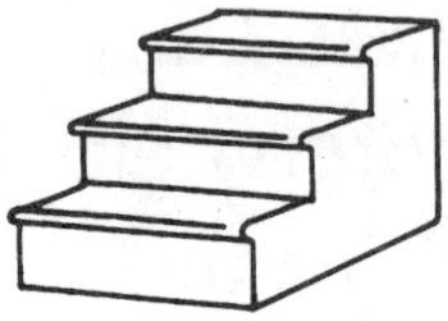 stars, stirs, stairs
10.  chirp, cheer, cheap	**11.**  bar, bore, bear	**12.**  peak, peer, plea

Read It Together A deer uses its ears to hear sounds in the forest.

Name ______________________________ Date ______________

High Frequency Words

Wish Upon a Star

Write a word from the box to complete each sentence.

High Frequency **Words**
five
four
made
men
night
second
such
thought
well
wish

Dear Grandpa,

I camped in a tent last ________. I ________ it would be scary, but it was ________ fun! Dad told me about ________ who studied the stars a long time ago. I could see four or ________ stars in the sky really well. I made a ________ upon one of them! Then I made a ________ one. I wished you could be here with us!

Your grandson,

Marcus

Name ________________________________ Date ______________

Grammar: Pronouns

Mix and Match Sentences

First choose a word or words from column A. Then choose a word from column B. Say a sentence using both parts and any other words you want to add. You may have to change the form of some of the words. After you say your sentence, have your partner replace the noun you chose with a pronoun and say the new sentence.

A	B
Ms. White	hat
The dogs	foot
A big tree	bike
The police officer's	house
Michael's	phone
A book	roar
A computer	gloves
A girl	coat
A man	car
Dad's	leaves
A lion	tail
The fish	head
A friend's	cover
Mom's	screen

Name ________________________ Date ____________

Phonics

Longer Words with *eer, ear*

Write the word that completes each sentence.

1. **nearby yearly sneering**

   My class went on a field trip to a ________ farm.

2. **dreary gears shearing**

   First, we saw a farmer ________ some sheep.

3. **sheer earmuffs dearly**

   I could hear sheep bleating, even with my ________ on!

4. **steer clear bleary**

   Next, we saw a big ________ in a field.

5. **wheelchair peering spear**

   When it looked up, I thought it was ________ at me!

6. **smear eerie earring**

   I thought that was sort of ________!

7. **cheery earlobe rearing**

   We saw a horse ________ up on its back legs.

8. **veer fear nearly**

   Another horse had to ________ out of the way!

9. **deer weary beard**

   We walked so much that I was ________ at the end of the day.

Name ______________________________ Date ______________

Grammar and Writing

Write Pronouns

Read the story. Then choose the word from the box that correctly completes each sentence.

I	she	him	us	his	herself

Some kids in Amber's class want to learn about the neighborhood. Amber tells herself that she knows whom they should see to learn about the neighborhood. ________ suggests they talk to Mr. Sanchez. The kids go to see ________ at his store. Amber opens the door and says, "Here we go. This store is ________." They ask Mr. Sanchez about all his memories of the neighborhood. "________ am so glad you talked about the neighborhood," Amber says. "Thank you so much for talking to ________."

Name ______________________ Date ____________

Grammar: Possessive Pronouns

Use Possessive Pronouns

Directions:

1. Play with two or three people. Copy all the words below onto separate cards.
2. Mix the cards up and put them facedown.
3. Turn over two cards and read them aloud. If the possessive pronoun card matches the noun card, keep both cards. If the two cards do not match, turn them facedown again in the same place.
4. The player with the most cards at the end wins.

Nouns			
Lee and Ana's notes	Our project	Lupe's and your plans	Lilu's marker
My goals	Your skill	Jackson's paper	

Possessive Pronouns			
Mine	Yours	Ours	Theirs
His	Hers	Yours	

Use three of the nouns above. Tell a partner something about yourself.

Name ______________________ Date ______________

Phonics

Prefixes *un-, re-, mis-*

Circle the word that names the picture.

1.
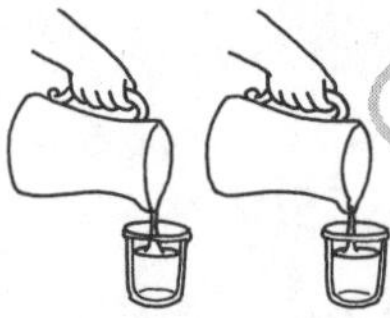
mistreat
refill
unfilled

2.

unhappy
retied
misread

3.
deg
dog
unpack
relock
misspell

4.

mismatch
rematch
unkind

5.
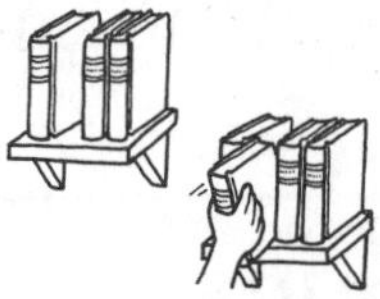
unload
mislead
replace

7.
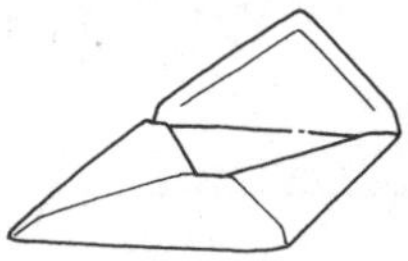
misname
resealed
unsealed

7.

mistake
unmade
remake

8.

undo
reset
misuse

9.

replay
unkind
misplace

10.

untied
retied
mistied

11.
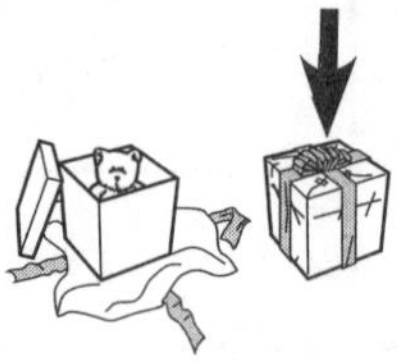
misstep
unsafe
rewrap

12.

unfolds
refolded
mistrust

Read It Together Mom is unhappy and replaces my mismatched socks.

Name ______________________ Date ______________

Character Map

Characters' Motives

Make a character map for the animal in your story.

Character	What the Character Does	What the Character is Like

Tell a partner your story. Then share your character map. Talk about the character's motives.

Name ______________________________ Date ______________

Phonics

Prefixes *un-, re-, mis-*

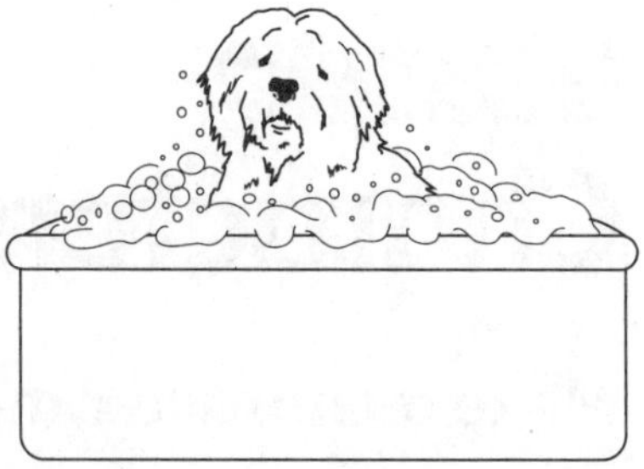

Write the word that completes each sentence.

1. **rename misuse unlike**

   My dog's name is Lucky, but I should __________ him Unlucky!

2. **unpaid reheated misjudged**

   Once he tried to jump over a stream, but he __________ his jump and landed with a big splash!

3. **rereads misplaces unties**

   He likes to play fetch, but he often __________ his stick.

4. **retrace misuse unzip**

   Then he has to __________ his steps until he finds it.

5. **misread refill unwise**

   Once Lucky was not very smart and did something that was

   __________.

6. **unfair mistake recall**

   He made a big __________ when he tried to play with a skunk.

7. **unfold misspell rewash**

   We gave him a bath and then had to ________ him for days!

8. **rewind unhappy misstep**

   He was __________ because he hates baths!

Word Cards: Words with *un-*, *re-*, *mis-*

 **unplug**	 **refill**	 **remail**	 **mismatch**
mistreat	**mistake**	**unseen**	**undo**
unsafe	**unwanted**	**resave**	**mistrust**
rename	**retake**	**unheard**	**unwind**
misbehave	**misread**	**restate**	**reawake**
unhurt	**misjudge**	**resend**	**misprint**
revote	**unasked**	**misspell**	**redo**

Spelling & Word Work

High Frequency Word Cards

get	move
buy	ball
old	few
just	eye
school	food
children	large
found	number
began	animal
another	often
together	might

Name ______________________ Date __________

Phonics

Suffixes *-y, -ly, -ful*

Circle the word that names the picture.

1.  carry careless careful	**2.**  muddy mindful mostly	**3.**  closely curly cheerful
4.  loudly lefty lapful	**5.**  cupful quickly quirky	**7.**  highly hungry helpful
7.  thickly thankful thirsty	**8.**  playful picky partly	**9.**  softly sandy forceful
10.  gently graceful grumpy	**11.**  windy wisely wishful	**12.**  skillful sleepy slowly

Read It Together My fluffy, playful kitten mews loudly.

Name ______________________________ Date ____________

High Frequency Words

Helping Out

Write a word from the box to complete each sentence.

High Frequency **Words**
animal
ball
eye
few
food
large
might
move
number
often

Dear Pedro,

I ________ be home late. Please help Grandma when you get home. First, feed each ________. The dog gets three large scoops of ________. The cat gets a different ________. She gets only one. Then take the dog outside. Throw a ________ a few times for the dog to fetch. Be careful that the cat doesn't get out the door. Keep your eye on her. She ________ sneaks out, and she can ________ fast!

Thank you,

Mom

Grammar: Past-Tense Verbs

Word Cards: Past Tense

add *-ed*	double consonant and add *-ed*	drop final silent *e* and add *-ed*	change *y* to *i* and add *-ed*
carry	dare	ask	like
water	watch	study	soak
grab	serve	check	show
try	use	snap	care
stop	move	worry	rub
pull	copy	surprise	hop

Name ______________________ Date __________

Phonics

Suffixes -y, -ly, -ful

Write the word with the correct suffix to complete each sentence.

1. wind

On a ________ day, Kelly flies her kite.

2. grace

She watches her ________ kite float through the sky.

3. quick

It swoops down ________ before it sails back up high.

4. snow

On a ________ day, Kelly goes sledding.

5. care

She is ________ on the hills.

6. safe

She sleds ________ where there are no trees.

7. rain

On a ________ day, Kelly stays inside.

8. close

She watches the rain ________.

9. hope

Kelly is ________ that the rain will stop soon so she can go outside to play.

Name ______________________ Date ____________

Grammar and Writing

Write Past-Tense Verbs

Read the story. Then choose the word from the word box that correctly completes each sentence. Write its past-tense form on the blank.

ask	copy	grab	like	show	worry

Yesterday, I __asked__ my uncle to help me make a birdhouse. He ________ his tool kit and came right over. I showed him my drawing that I ________ from a book. First, we got some wood. Then he ________ me how to measure the pieces. I ________ that I could not cut the pieces straight, so he cut them for me. Soon, the birdhouse was finished. We both really ________ the new birdhouse.

Name ____________________ Date ____________

Character Map

Go to Sleep, Gecko!

Make a character map for the characters in "Go to Sleep, Gecko!"

Character	What the Character Does	What the Character is Like
Gecko	He complains about the fireflies.	He can't sleep.

Share your character map with a partner. Compare what you wrote about the characters in "Go to Sleep, Gecko!"

Name ______________________ Date ______________

Phonics

Words with *oo, ea, ou*

Cut out the words and sort them. Use the words in sentences.

wood	feather
took	weather
stood	steady
brook	touch
cookie	young
breath	cousin

Name ______________________ Date __________

Phonics

Words with *oo, ea, ou*

Write the words to complete each sentence.

1. **cook young**

   Dad started to ________ when he was a ________ boy.

2. **cookbooks read**

   He ________ Grandma's ________ and chose things to make.

3. **look books**

   Now other people ________ for food to make in ________ that Dad writes.

4. **instead breakfast**

   Sometimes Dad makes eggs for ________, but this morning he made oatmeal ________.

5. **good bread**

   He made some ________ that was really ________, too.

6. **cousin took**

   First I ________ a taste, and then my ________ did.

7. **shook head**

   He ________ his ________, patted his tummy, and said, "Yum!"

Name ______________________________ Date ____________

Phonics

Words with *gh*

Unscramble each word and write it. Then write a sentence using the word.

1. g o r u h r o u g h This sand feels rough.	**2. t g t i h** _ _ _ _ _
3. h a g s n _ _ _ _ _	**4. u h t o g** _ _ _ _ _
5. h e u n o g _ _ _ _ _ _	**7. r g b i h t** _ _ _ _ _ _
7. y r h g l u o _ _ _ _ _ _ _	**8. s g i i h g n** _ _ _ _ _ _ _

Word Cards: Words with *oo, ea, ou*

 cookie	 book	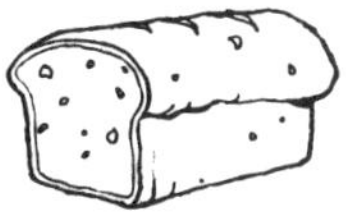 bread	 couple
young	enough	read	look
notebook	cousin	rookie	dead
rough	rook	touch	double
thread	health	hook	meadow
cook	shook	instead	nook
head	country	trouble	tough

Spelling & Word Work

High Frequency Word Cards

line	room
done	head
side	small
try	pick
once	own
must	stay
next	along
funny	change
follow	sometimes
laugh	enough

Name ______________________ Date ______________

Comparison Chart

Compare Genres

Complete the comparison chart to show how the selections are the same and different.

"Go to Sleep, Gecko!"	"Enric Sala: Marine Ecologist"
• folk tale • fiction	• folk tale • fiction

Use your comparison chart to tell a partner how "Go to Sleep, Gecko!" and "Enric Sala: Marine Ecologist" are alike and different.

Name ______________________________ Date ______________

Phonics

Words with *au, aw*

Circle the word that names the picture.

1. 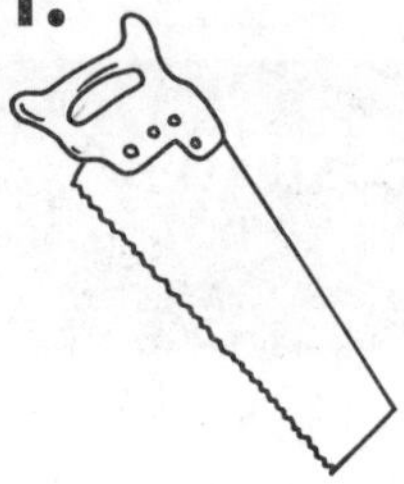 sea saw sat	**2.** 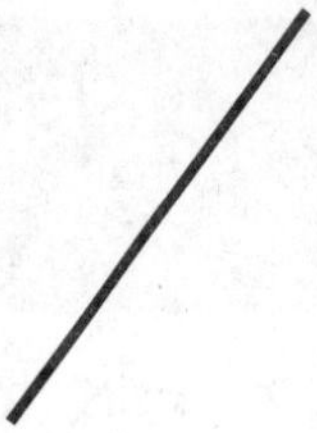 line lawn loan	**3.**  ray raw row
4.  claw clap clear	**5.**  pen paw pea	**6.** 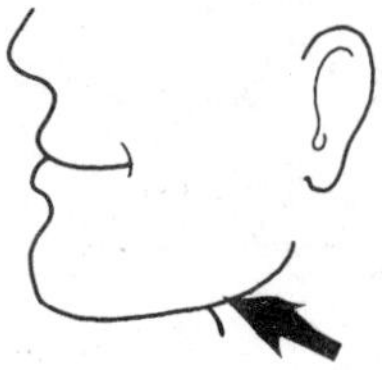 jaw jam jug
7.  deep draw dad	**8.**  hike hawk heat	**9.**  lump lawn lamp
10.  road raw rod	**11.**  pie pin prawn	**12.**  crawl crane crow

Read It Together Paul and his dog saw a hawk along the road.

Name ________________________ Date ____________

High Frequency Words

Watch Them Grow!

Write a word from the box to complete each sentence.

High Frequency **Words**
along
change
enough
head
own
pick
room
small
sometimes
stay

1. We have just ________ room to have two pear trees in the backyard.

2. The trees are still ________, but pears grow on them.

3. I like to watch the pears get bigger and ________ as they grow.

4. Most of the pears ________ on the branches, but sometimes they fall.

5. Once a ripe yellow pear fell and hit me right on the top of my ________!

6. I like it when the end of summer comes ________.

7. Then I can ________ my own pears to eat!

Name ________________________ Date ____________

Grammar: Irregular Past-Tense Verbs

Use Irregular Verbs

1. To play, take turns with a partner.
2. Toss a marker onto the game board.
3. Say a sentence with the present-tense verb you land on. Then say the past-tense verb and use it in a sentence to tell about the past.

do	go
says	sing
give	takes

Name ______________________________ Date ______________

Phonics

Words with *au, aw*

Write the words to complete each sentence.

1. yawned dawn

Mai woke up at __________ and __________.

2. saw fawn

She looked outside and __________ a __________.

3. lawn tawny

The __________ animal was eating weeds on her __________.

4. sauntered paused

When Mai went outside, the animal __________ and then __________ back into the woods.

5. claws hawk

Mai saw a __________ swoop down and grab food in its __________.

6. launched hauled

Then it __________ itself back up into the sky and __________ its food away.

7. because draw

Mai ran back inside __________ she wanted to __________ the animals.

Name ______________________ Date __________

Grammar and Writing

Write Irregular Verbs

Read the letter. Then write the word from the word box that correctly completes each sentence.

begin	come	do	give	go
began	came	did	gave	went

Dear Grandpa,

This is what we ___did___ in school last week. Every kid decided to be an animal. Then we each ________ a talk about the animal we were. We all ________ turns telling about ourselves. My friend Sarah ________ first. She was a penguin. She was great. She ________ to talk about all the raw fish she liked to eat. Then my turn ________. I was a tiger!

Love,

Marike

Name ______________________ Date ____________

Grammar: Past-Tense Verbs

Use Past-Tense Verbs

Grammar Rules Past-Tense Verbs

- Add *-ed* to most verbs when you talk about a past action. Example: *kick* + *-ed* = *kicked*
- Some verbs have special forms to show an action in the past. Example: *say* → *said*

Circle the correct verb form.

1. Gecko want/wanted to sleep that night.

2. Gecko goed/went to see Elephant.

3. Elephant talks/talked to the fireflies last week.

4. The fireflies seed/saw Elephant coming.

5. Gecko sayed/said everything was okay.

Use the past tense of *is* or *are* in a sentence about Gecko.

Name ______________________ Date ____________

Phonics

Words with *al, all*

Circle the word that names the picture.

1. 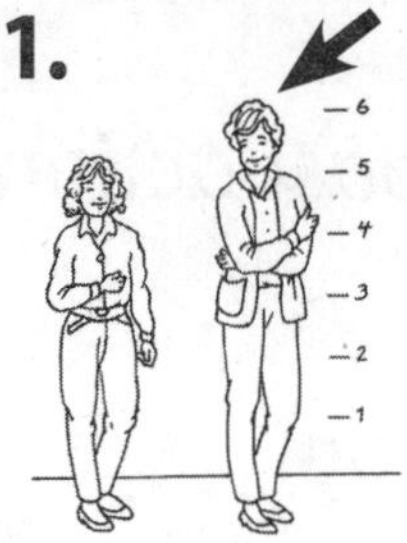 tell tail tall	**2.** 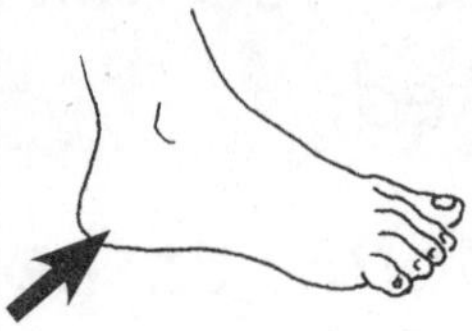 hill hall heel	**3.** 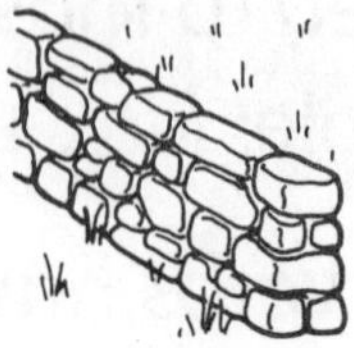 will wall well
4. 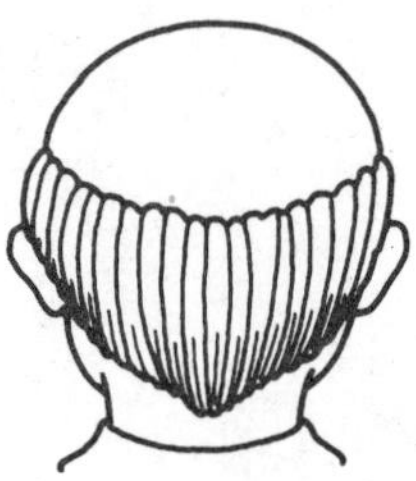 bald bold bell	**5.**  bell bill ball	**6.**  fall fill feel
7.  small smell smile	**8.**  sale salt seal	**9.** 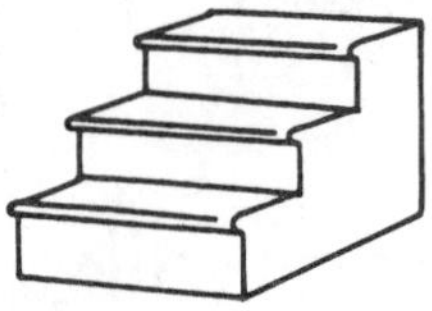 stair store steer
10. 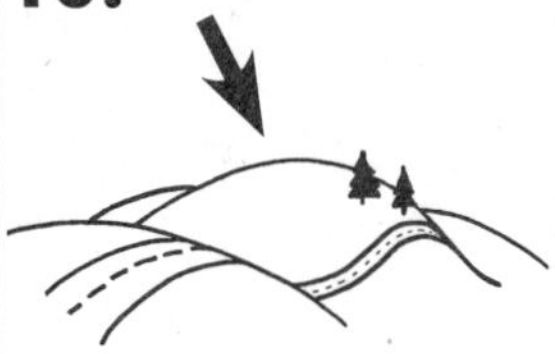 hail heel hill	**11.**  cool call curl	**12.**  hall hat heat

Read It Together Walk by the tall wall. Did the ball fall there?

Name ________________________________ Date ______________

Topic and Main Idea Chart

Topic and Main Idea

Work with a partner. What nonfiction selection have you both read? Find the topic and main idea of the selection. Then fill out the chart.

Topic	Main Idea

Use your chart to discuss the topic and main idea of your selection.

Name ______________________ Date ____________

Phonics

Words with *al, all*

Write the words to complete each sentence.

1. mall Hall

Mrs. ________ and her family took a trip to the ________.

2. stalls hallway

People were selling goods from ________ in the ________.

3. baseballs bald

A ________ man was selling ________.

4. ball always

Billy ________ wanted to have his very own ________.

5. wallet almost

He looked in his ________ and saw that he had ________ enough cash.

6. all tallest

His ________ sister looked at ________ her cash.

7. smallest also

His ________ sister ________ looked in her purse.

8. baseball all

Together, they had ________ the cash Billy needed to get a new ________!

Spelling & Word Work

Word Cards: Words with *al, all*

 salt	 bald	 ball	 almond
Walt	basket-ball	mall	football
hallway	almost	wall	always
tall	fall	scald	hallway
salty	halt	squalls	volleyball
small	call	stall	waltz
false	malted	also	alter

Spelling & Word Work

High Frequency Word Cards

boy	ride
us	close
pull	sleep
gave	cry
took	show
myself	green
upon	plant
brother	hurt
sister	jump
always	please

Name ______________________ Date __________

Phonics

Words with *oi, oy*

Circle the word that names the picture.

1.  corn coin cone	**2.**  oil old eel	**3.**  pot paint point
4.  box boy bee	**5.**  toy tea top	**7.**  nose noise nice
7.  teeth toast toys	**8.**  boil bake book	**9.** 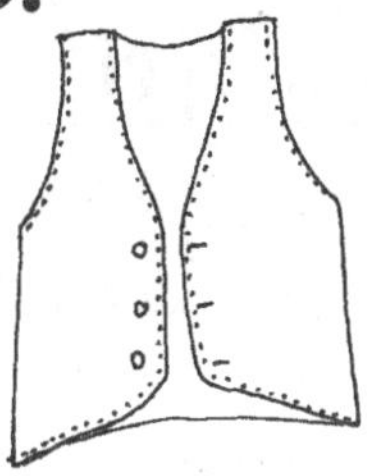 vase voice vest
10.  spoil spot speed	**11.**  sail soil sell	**12.**  coil coat cat

Read It Together Point to the toys that make the most noise.

Name ______________________ Date ____________

High Frequency Words

The Boat Ride

Write a word from the box to complete each sentence.

High Frequency **Words**
close
cry
green
hurt
jump
plant
please
ride
show
sleep

My family and I ________ to the beach on a boat. Some gulls are flying ________ to the boat. I show them some bread, and they ________ out. They seem to say, "Will you ________ share your bread with us?" I put bread on the railing and step back. The gulls fly down. I jump, but they don't ________ me. They just take the bread from the railing! I sit in the sun, close my eyes, and go to ________. When I wake up, I see a big ________ plant on the shoreline and know that we are almost at the beach!

Name ______________________________ Date ______________

Grammar: Future-Tense Verbs

Use Future-Tense Verbs with *Will*

Directions:

1. Make a spinner.
2. Play with a partner.
3. Take turns spinning the spinner.
4. Read the words. Say a sentence using a contraction for the words you land on. Then have your partner say your sentence without the contraction.

Make a Spinner

1. Put a paper clip in the center of the circle.
2. Hold one end of the paper clip with a pencil.
3. Spin the paper clip around the pencil.

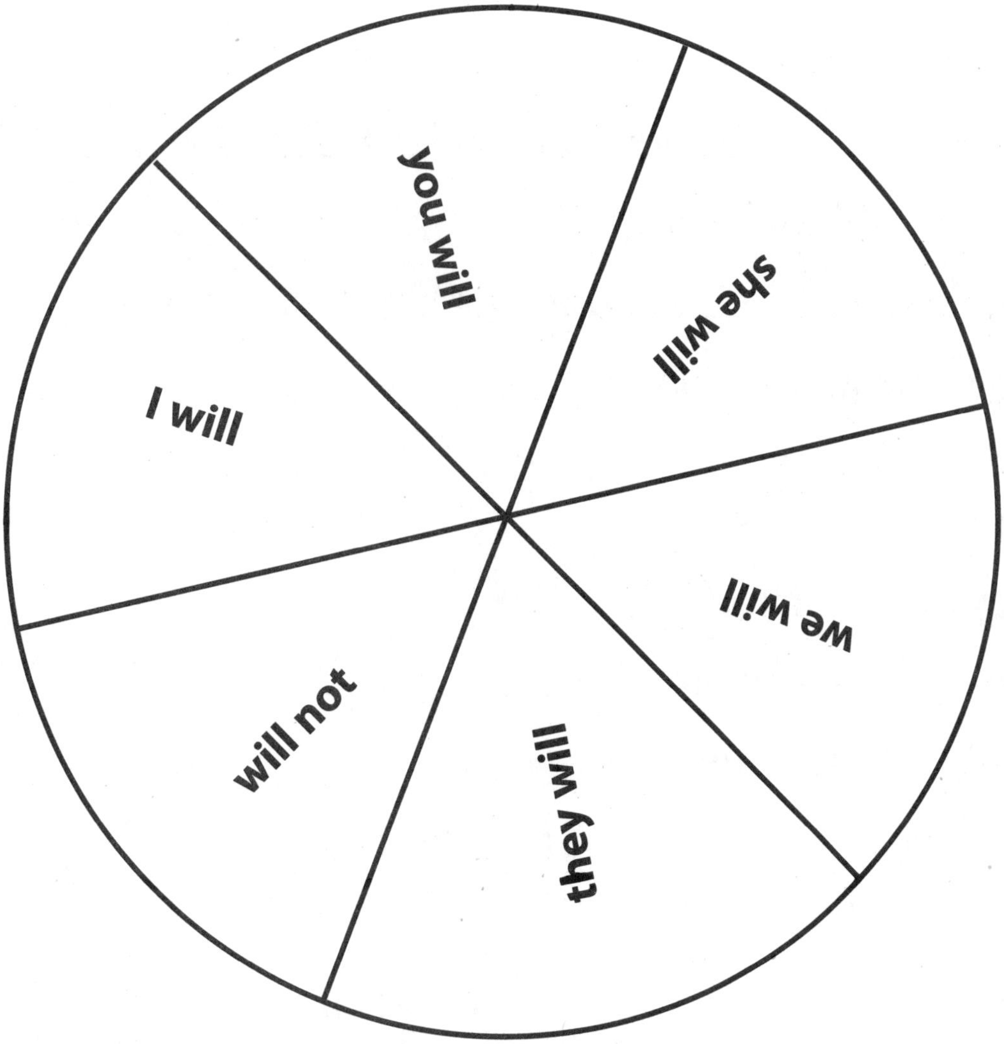

Name ______________________ Date ____________

Phonics

Words with *oi, oy*

Write the word that completes each sentence.

1. **enjoy newsboy oil**

   What do you ________ doing on a hot day?

2. **oyster soil voice**

   Joy plants seeds in the ________ in her garden.

3. **royal point moist**

   She must keep the dirt ________ so the seeds will grow.

4. **joins joyful loyal**

   Troy ________ his pals at the field in a nearby park.

5. **spoil sirloin noisy**

   They play a ________ game of baseball.

6. **toy broiling joint**

   When they get ________ hot, they jump into the swimming pool at the park.

7. **soy coil choice**

   Roy makes a different ________.

8. **boil coins noise**

   He takes some ________ from his piggybank.

9. **boy foil pointing**

   Then the happy ________ rides his bike to the ice cream shop!

Name ______________________ Date ______________

Grammar and Writing

Write Future-Tense Verbs with *Will*

Read the story. Then choose the word from the word box that correctly completes each sentence.

he'll it'll we'll I'll won't they'll

Our class is going to the zoo. I am sure we'll have a fantastic time. I love the monkeys. I hope ________ do lots of funny things. Mr. Dean, our teacher, says ________ tell us about the different animals. I hope the weather is good. ________ be great if the sun shines. It ________ be as good if it rains, but the zoo trip will still be fun. ________ tell you all about it!

Name ______________________ Date ____________

Vocabulary

Yes or No?

1. **Listen to the questions. Write the Key Word where it belongs in each sentence.**
2. **Listen to the questions again.**
3. **Write yes or no for each question.**

1. Do animals in the wild hide from danger ? yes

2. Are cleaner shrimp and oxpeckers animal ________ ? ________

3. Can animals ________ each other? ________

4. Is a plover ________ to a honeyguide bird? ________

5. Are the clownfish and sea anemone ________ partners? ________

6. Does a badger have the ________ to help a coyote? ________

Name ______________________________ Date ______________

Topic and Main Idea Chart

Odd Couples

FIll out the topic and main idea chart for "Odd Couples."

Topic:	**Main Idea:** Animal partnerships help both animals survive.

Detail: Cleaner shrimp keep other fish clean.
Detail:

Use your topic and main idea chart to tell a partner about "Odd Couples."

Name ______________________ Date ____________

Phonics

Words with *ow, ou*

Unscramble each word and write it. Then write a sentence using the word.

1. o l u d l o u d I hear a loud noise. ________________	**2. o n d w** __ __ __ __ ________________ ________________
3. w l h o __ __ __ __ ________________ ________________	**4. d l c u o** __ __ __ __ __ ________________ ________________
5. t u c o n __ __ __ __ __ ________________ ________________	**6. d w o c r** __ __ __ __ __ ________________ ________________
7. n f w r o __ __ __ __ __ ________________ ________________	**8. o g n u r d** __ __ __ __ __ __ ________________ ________________

Name ______________________ Date __________

Phonics

Words with *ow, ou*

Write the words to complete each sentence.

1. now downtown

Right ________ Dad and I are ________ at the circus.

2. surrounds round

A big, ________ tent ________ us.

3. crowd shouts

The ________ claps and ________ at all the circus acts.

4. frown clown

I like the funny ________ with a huge, red ________ for a mouth.

5. cowboy flower

He wears a ________ hat with a red ________ on top.

6. hound crouches

He ________ down low and pretends to be a ________ that is howling.

7. brown crowns

Dad likes the ________ horses wearing ________ on their heads.

8. thousand drowsy

By the end, I am ________, but I wish I could come back a ________ more times!

Word Cards: Words with *ou, ow*

 hound	 pound	 tower	 flower
count	pounce	found	towel
power	wow	howl	loud
under-ground	shower	sound	around
crowd	town	down	ground
hour	about	round	pout
frown	crowded	vow	downtown

Spelling & Word Work

High Frequency Word Cards

made	will
five	soon
four	black
men	brown
night	group
such	high
well	leave
wish	study
second	open
thought	point

Name ______________________ Date ____________

Comparison Chart

Compare Topics and Main Ideas

Complete the comparison chart to compare "Odd Couples" and "Working Together."

Title	Topic	Main Idea
"Odd Couples"		
"Working Together"		

Use the comparison chart to explain the topic and main idea of each selection.

Name ______________________________ Date ______________

Phonics

Words with Schwa

Circle the word that names the picture.

1.  await abrupt asleep	**2.** 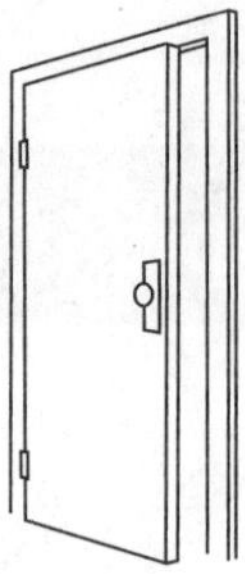 alive ajar ago	**3.**  along adult anew
4.  amazed around amount	**5.**  awake along awhile	**6.**  aloud agree alone
7.  avoid ashore ashes	**8.** 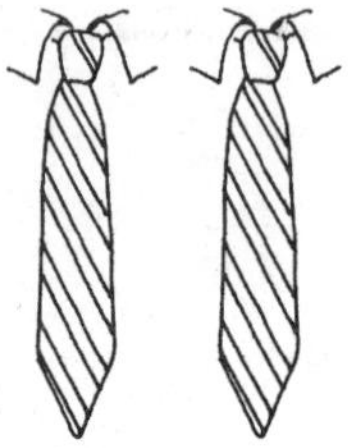 afraid alert alike	**9.**  alarm away alright
10.  ahead appear adore	**11.**  aware afoot afloat	**12.**  account across annoy

Read It Together Are you awake or asleep after your alarm rings?

Name ______________________________ Date ______________

High Frequency Words

At the Lighthouse

Write a word from the box to complete each sentence.

High Frequency Words
black
brown
group
high
leave
open
point
soon
study
will

1. When you ________ the bus stop, turn left on the first street.
2. Walk to the ________ where Hill Street meets Rocky Road, and you will see a brown house with a black door.
3. Turn right, and ________ you will come to a lighthouse.
4. Walk up the stairs to the top, and you will be ________ above the world!
5. You can look out over the ________ sea!
6. You might see a ________ of sea birds fly by.
7. You can ________ these birds to find out about them.

Word Cards: Future-Tense Verbs

tell	watch	eat	give
visit	hunt	make	see
need	fly	stop	start
study	swim	sit	leave
help	look	catch	use
clean	ride	play	stay
ask	give	walk	buy

Name ______________________ Date ____________

Phonics

Words with Schwa

Write the words to complete each sentence.

1. alarm awake

I'm wide ________ when my ________ goes off.

2. awhile across

I wait ________ and then run ________ the house to find Mom and Dad.

3. asleep appear

They ________ to be ________.

4. aloud aware

So I yell ________, "Are you ________ of the time?"

5. about annoyed

"It's only ________ seven o'clock, isn't it?" says Dad. He sounds a little ________.

6. awaiting away

It's later than that, and I've been ________ this day for a long time. I don't go ________.

7. alone agree

Finally I ________ to leave them ________ until nine.

8. adore arrive

At ten o'clock, we ________ at the dog pound, and I choose my new puppy. I ________ her!

Name ______________________________ Date ______________

Grammar and Writing

Write Future-Tense Verbs

Read the email. Then choose the word or words from the box that correctly complete each sentence. Write the words.

will	is going	she's	are going	am	you're

Hey Jason,

I have got some cool news! My mom got a new job at the zoo. Mom is going to start next month. ________ going to be the new assistant beekeeper. I ________ going to visit the zoo and learn all about the bees. Mom ________ show me how the bees make honey. Of course, ________ going to come with me. You and I ________ to have a great time at the zoo!

Pablo

Name ______________________ Date ____________

Grammar: Future Tense

Say Future-Tense Verbs

Directions:

1. Play with a partner.
2. Spin the spinner.
3. Change the verb to show the future tense. Say a sentence using the future-tense verb.

Make a Spinner

1. Put a paper clip in the center of the circle.
2. Hold one end of the paper clip with a pencil.
3. Spin the paper clip around the pencil.

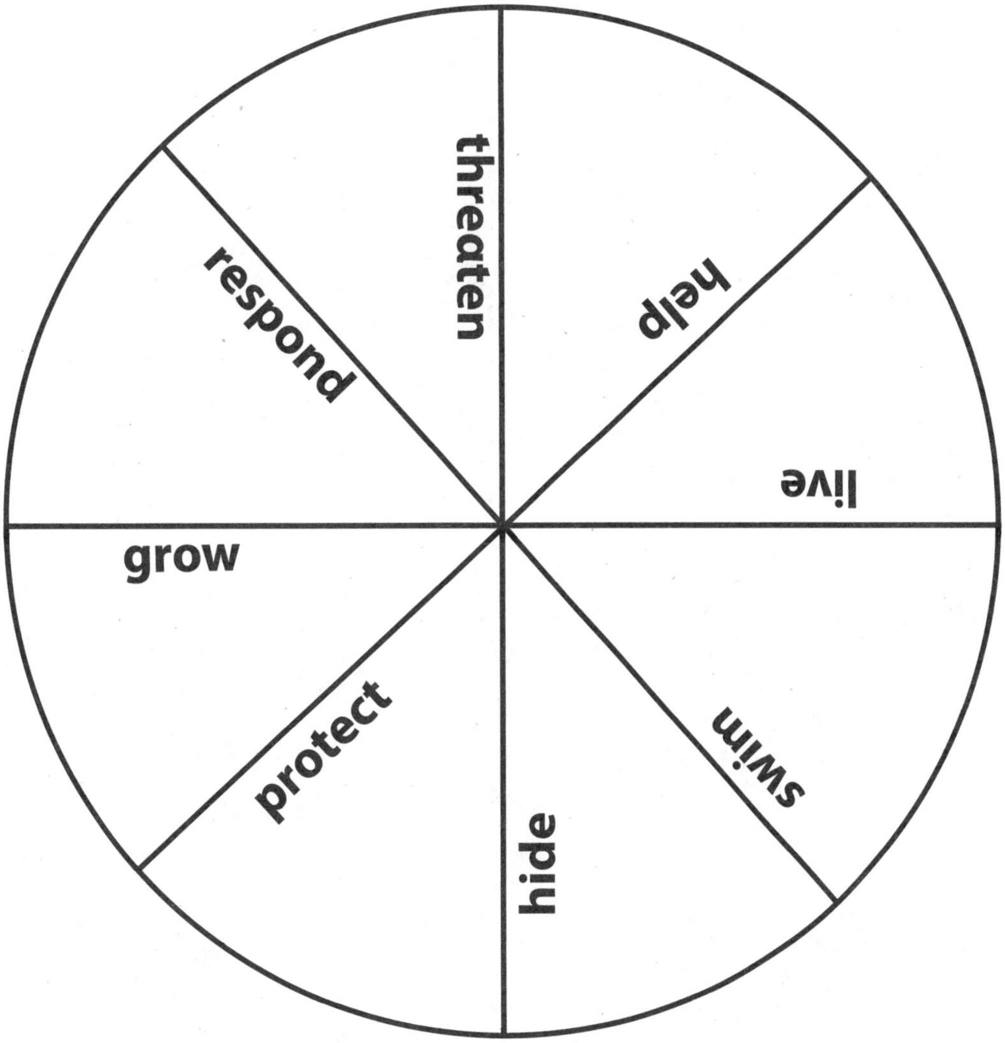

Name ______________________ Date ____________

Phonics

Prefixes *dis-, pre-, in-, im-*

Cut out the cards. Match cards to make words. Then use each word in a sentence.

dis	**teen**
pre	**heat**
in	**put**
im	**land**
like	**perfect**
appear	**polite**

Name ______________________ Date ____________

Character Map

Characters' Feelings

Make a character map to tell how a character feels and why.

Character	How the Character Feels	Why the Character Feels This Way

Use your character map to tell a partner about a character's feelings in a story that you like.

Name ______________________ Date ____________

Phonics

Prefixes *dis-, pre-, in-, im-*

Write the word that completes each sentence.

1. distrust preschool indoors

Cole and Rosa have to stay ________ today because it is raining.

2. disagree impolite incomplete

At first they ________ about what to do, but then they decide to make cookies.

3. precut incorrect immigrate

Rosa thinks Cole likes peanut butter cookies, but she is ________.

4. inputs prepays dislikes

Cole ________ peanut butter, so they decide to make oatmeal cookies.

5. disarmed pregame imperfect

They don't want the cookies to be ________, so they work carefully.

6. implant preplan insight

They ________ and prepare before they begin.

7. indirect improper disappear

After the cookies are baked, they ________ quickly! Yum!

Spelling & Word Work

Words with Prefixes *dis-, pre-, im-, in-*

 display	 preschool	 impossible	 inside
disagree	disrespect	immature	inhuman
prepay	indecent	preview	immobile
impolite	disorder	imperfect	informal
disservice	improper	disapprove	prejudge
infield	incorrect	pregame	dissatisfied
precook	preorder	insecure	impatient

High Frequency Word Cards

move	seem
ball	word
few	read
eye	learn
food	idea
large	father
number	mother
animal	country
often	picture
might	America

Name ____________________ Date ____________

Phonics

Suffixes *-er, -or, -less, -ness*

Circle the word that names the picture.

1.  brainless brightness baker	**2.**  farmer fearless fondness	**3.**  trainer tractor truthless
4.  darkness dancer dodger	**5.**  hardness hunter hopeless	**7.**  supper slowness swimmer
7.  dryness doctor danger	**8.**  sailor singer sadness	**9.**  thicker thinker timeless
10.  batter boneless blackness	**11.**  spineless spotless speaker	**12.**  kicker cordless kindness

Read It Together The sailor is a fearless swimmer.

Name ______________________ Date ____________

High Frequency Words

A New Home

Write a word from the box to complete each sentence.

High Frequency **Words**
America
country
father
idea
learn
mother
picture
read
seem
word

Dear Grandma and Grandpa,

Here is a ________ of my father, my mother, and me. We are in our new ________, the United States of America. I ________ new things in school every day. I can ________ in English now. I teach myself at least one new English ________ every day. I am happy, and Mom and Dad ________ happy, too. I have a great ________! Can you come and visit us soon? I miss you!

Your grandson,

Hector

Grammar: Prepositions

Word Cards: Prepositions

above	behind	in	in front of
at	beside	on	under
flag	door	parade	picnic
lunch	sky	car	band
birthday	fireworks	party	food
milk	pie	table	customers
roof	window	chairs	horses
people	house	street	float

Name ______________________ Date ____________

Phonics

Suffixes *-er, -or, -less, -ness*

Write the word that completes each sentence.

1. **fondness careless tractor**

   Dale has a ________ for the sea.

2. **helpless brightness sailor**

   That's why he wants to be a ________ when he grows up.

3. **rancher cloudless actor**

   He wants to travel under ________ skies.

4. **joyless diver dryness**

   Maybe he will also be a ________ who explores life under the water.

5. **richness painter useless**

   He will learn about the ________ of life in the sea.

6. **settler visitor darkness**

   Maybe he will study life in the ________ at the bottom.

7. **cordless teacher lightless**

   It is ________ down where the sun doesn't shine!

8. **worker harmless moistness**

   What kind of ________ would you like to be when you grow up?

9. **greenness hairless countless**

   You have ________ jobs to choose from!

Name ______________________ Date ____________

Grammar and Writing

Write Prepositions

Read the story. Then choose the word from the box that correctly completes each sentence.

above	behind	beside	in	on	under

I watched the Fourth of July parade last week. I watched it sitting beside my parents. The parade was ________ Main Street. My sister plays in the high school band. The band marched ________ the parade. We waited for the band. The sky ________ us was very clear. I got really hot. Mom gave me a cold drink from the cooler ________ her chair. Then, we finally saw my sister. She was playing the trumpet. She was marching ________ a boy playing a drum.

Name ______________________ Date ____________

Character Map

Apple Pie 4th of July

Make a character map for the characters in "Apple Pie 4th of July."

Character	How the Character Feels	Why the Character Feels This Way
The girl telling the story	Unhappy	She thinks no one will want Chinese food on the Fourth of July.

Use your character map to describe the story characters to a partner.

Name ____________________ Date ____________

Phonics

Final Syllable Consonant + *le*

Circle the word that names the picture.

1.  able apple anthill	**2.** 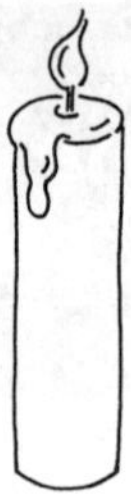 candle candy cuddle	**3.**  pebble paddle puzzle
4.  bottle bottom bumble	**5.** 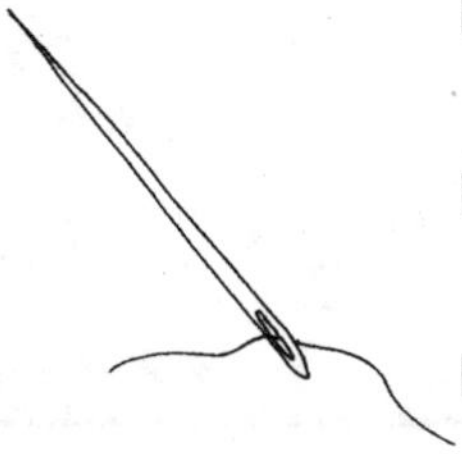 needy nibble needle	**6.**  bundle bunny bubble
7. 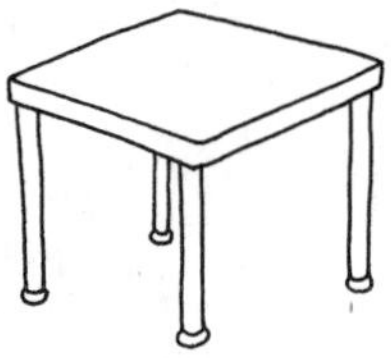 tattle table trouble	**8.**  cattle crackle cable	**9.** 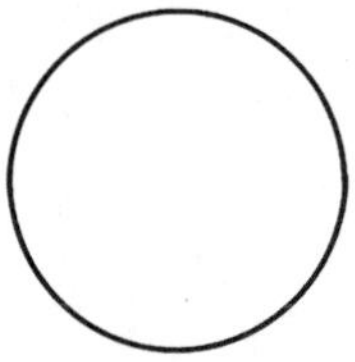 cradle circus circle
10.  purple poodle puddle	**11.**  little laundry lentil	**12.**  turtle tunnel tangle

Read It Together Would you put an apple or cattle on a table?

Name ______________________ Date ____________

Phonics

Final Syllable Consonant + *le*

Write the word that completes each sentence.

1. **maples riddles giggles**

   Can you answer these ________?

2. **turtle cradle sprinkle**

   I am a reptile, and I have a shell. I am a ________.

3. **handle gentle poodle**

   I am a dog, and I have curly fur. I am a ________.

4. **apple uncle eagle**

   I fly high in the sky because I am a bird. I am an ________.

5. **beetle title noodle**

   I am a small bug with a shell. I am a ________.

6. **fiddles pebbles wiggles**

   We are small rocks. We are ________.

7. **rattle bubble saddle**

   You put me on a horse before you ride. I am a ________.

8. **fizzle jungle gobble**

   I am where tigers and monkeys live. I am the ________.

9. **purple sparkle cuddle**

   You get me if you mix red and blue paint. I am ________.

Spelling & Word Work

Word Cards: Words with C + *le*

 eagle	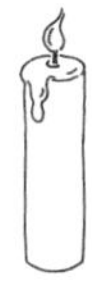 candle	 turtle	 puzzle
purple	middle	silly	finally
squeal	skillet	candy	stable
single	fable	let	pale
example	crate	maple	bridle
quilt	rifle	pellet	whale
rally	gentle	noble	steeple

Spelling & Word Work

High Frequency Word Cards

room	got
head	tell
small	story
pick	sing
own	song
stay	music
along	still
change	state
sometimes	today
enough	example

Name ______________________ Date ____________

Comparison Chart

Compare Language

Compare the language in "Apple Pie 4th of July" and "America: A Weaving." Write what the sentences or phrases mean.

"Apple Pie 4th of July"	"America: A Weaving"
I hear the parade passing by. This means exactly what it says.	America, America, a never-ending weaving! Meaning: Many cultures and traditions make America.
My parents do not understand all American things.	

Take turns with a partner. Explain which words mean exactly what they say and which words do not.

Name ______________________________ Date ______________

Phonics

Final Syllables *-tion, -ture*

Circle the word that names the picture.

1.  vulture value vacation	**2.** $\frac{1}{2}$ fiction fracture fraction	**3.** ? queenly question quotation
4.  potter potion pasture	**5.**  noodle nation nowhere	**7.**  posture picture pebble
7.  caption capture caution	**8.**  lotion lecture ladle	**9.**  notion nature never
10.  traction teacher texture	**11.**  section scary sculpture	**12.**  station stature stampede

Read It Together The structure near the pasture is a bus station.

Name ______________________ Date ____________

High Frequency Words

Story Time

Write a word from the box to complete each sentence.

High Frequency Words
example
got
music
sing
song
state
still
story
tell
today

1. Morgan goes to summer camp in the ________ of New York.

2. Every Sunday night is music night. The campers sit in a circle and ________ camp songs.

3. Every Friday night is story night. A camper can ________ any kind of story.

4. For ________, Morgan told a spooky story last Friday night.

5. Some campers ________ scared when Morgan told her story.

6. They ________ jump when they hear loud noises!

7. It is Friday ________. What story would you tell the other campers?

Name ______________________ Date ______________

Grammar: Prepositions

Use Prepositions

Directions:

1. **Make a spinner.**
2. **Play with a partner.**
3. **Take turns spinning the spinner.**
4. **Read the word. Say a sentence using the preposition you land on. Then have your partner say whether the preposition in your sentence shows time or direction.**

Make a Spinner

1. Put a paper clip in the center of the circle.
2. Hold one end of the paper clip with a pencil.
3. Spin the paper clip around the pencil.

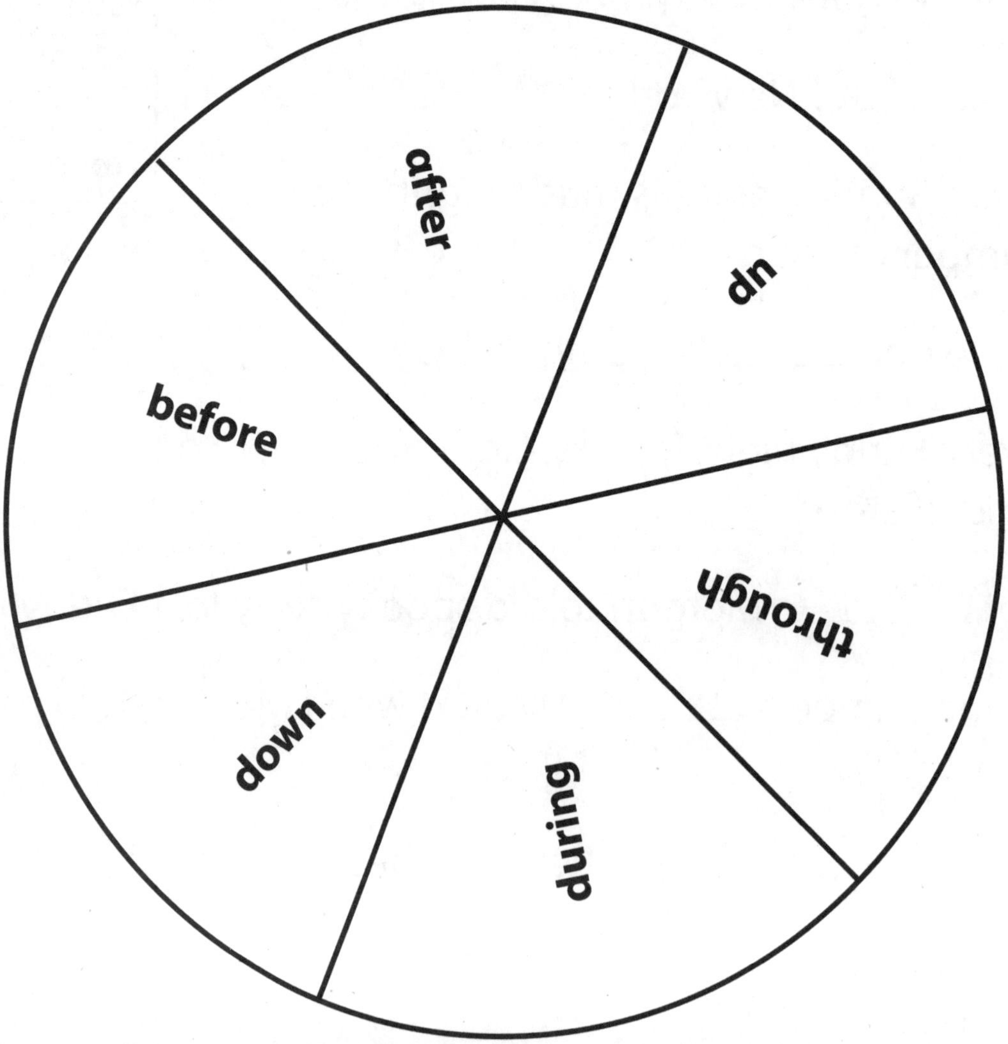

Name ______________________ Date ____________

Phonics

Final Syllables *-tion, -ture*

Write the word that completes each sentence.

1. **education moisture lotion**

   The children at Pine Street School get a great ________.

2. **nation instruction capture**

   Teachers give them ________ in a lot of subjects.

3. **section caption addition**

   In math class, they learn ________ and subtraction.

4. **mixture fiction furniture**

   In English class, they read books that are ________.

5. **pictures lectures portions**

   In art class, they paint different kinds of ________.

6. **question mention nature**

   The students go outside to study ________.

7. **attention futures creatures**

   They see many living ________.

8. **fraction vulture donation**

   Once they saw a ________ circling in the sky.

9. **cultures stations features**

   They learned that a bald head is one of its ________.

Name ______________________ Date __________

Phonics

Final Syllables *-sion, -cian*

Write the words to complete each sentence.

1. **mansion musician**

   A ________ lives in that huge ________.

2. **electrician television**

   She calls an ________ to help her with the wires for her new ________.

3. **permission magician**

   Then she gives her friend the ________ her ________ to perform a show.

4. **decision admission**

   The friends make a ________ to give children free ________ to the show.

5. **division sessions**

   So many children come that there is a ________ of the show into two ________.

6. **expression musician**

   In one, the ________ plays music with ________.

7. **magician vision**

   In the other, the ________ plays tricks on the children's ________.

Name ______________________ Date ____________

Grammar and Writing

Write Prepositions

Read the story. Then write the word from the box that correctly completes each sentence.

across	before	through	after	to	down

Welcome to our special celebration of America. Did you walk ___to___ the park or ride in a car? You can walk to many exhibits ________ the hill. You can get your lunch ticket in the big tent. Be sure to go there ________ lunch. To find the international café, walk ________ the bridge. ________ lunch, you can see the exhibits. To get to the exhibits, go ________ the gates.

Name ______________________ Date ____________

Grammar: Prepositions

Use Prepositions

Grammar Rules Prepositions

Some prepositions show location.	→	in, on, above, over, below, under, beside, next to
Some prepositions show direction.	→	up, down, through, across, into, around

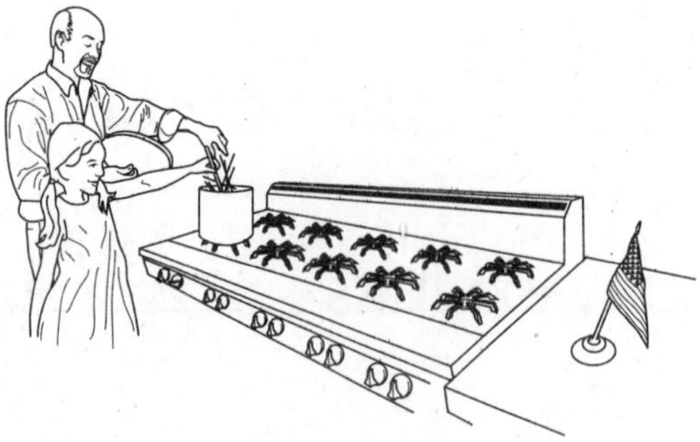

Circle the word to complete each sentence. Then read the sentence.

1. The pot is under/on the stove.

2. Dad puts noodles into/across the pot.

3. I stand next to/above Dad.

4. I stir the noodles around/down with a spoon.

5. The flag is beside/through the stove.

Write a sentence that includes a preposition. Share your sentence with a partner.

Name ______________________________ Date ______________

Phonics

Words with Schwa

Circle the word that names the picture.

1.  gerbil gallon **garden**	**2.**  person pardon pencil	**3.**  puffin parcel pretzel
4.  ribbon royal reason	**5.**  shovel station shorten	**6.**  wiggle wagon waken
7. 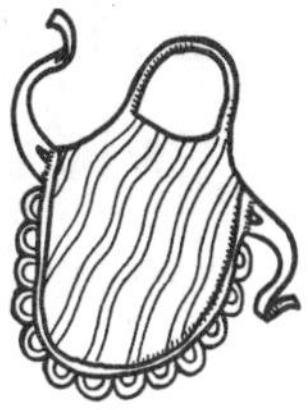 apple apron action	**8.**  squirrel shorten squirted	**9.** 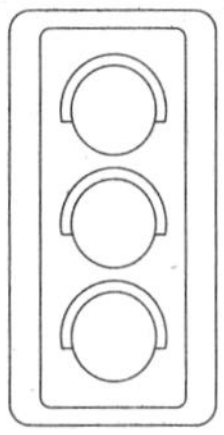 satin slogan signal
10.  jacket jackal juggle	**11.**  channel chisel chicken	**12.**  seven sandal season

Read It Together Do you wear an apron, a sandal, or a ribbon on your foot?

Name ______________________ Date ____________

Author's Purpose Chart

Author's Purpose

Make an author's purpose chart to tell about a nonfiction text you have read.

Clues from the Title:	Clues from the Kind of Writing:
Author's Purpose	
Clues from the Details:	**Clues from the Main Idea:**

Share your chart with a partner and compare authors' purposes.

Name ______________________ Date ____________

Phonics

Words with Schwa

Write the words to complete each sentence.

1. person medal

My grandma is a ________ who should get a ________.
She does everything!

2. kitchen apron

Sometimes she puts on her ________ and makes goodies in the ________.

3. muffins lemon

She is a baker. She bakes the best ________ ________!

4. mitten woolen

She is a knitter. She knits warm ________ things. Each hat and ________ is perfect!

5. musical vocal

She is a ________ star in ________ shows in the city.

6. wooden model

Grandma is a ________ maker. We make ________ airplanes together.

7. petal garden

When she works in her ________, Grandma is like a farmer. She knows every ________ and leaf on her plants.

Spelling & Word Work

Word Cards: Words with Schwa

 sailor	 flower	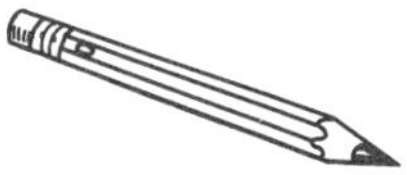 pencil	 capital
kitchen	player	mother	gallon
flavor	cotton	fallen	Megan
nickel	payer	father	signal
listen	Mexican	council	button
kicker	cellar	teacher	American
chicken	carol	evil	pretzel

Spelling & Word Work

High Frequency Word Cards

ride	big
close	home
sleep	new
cry	bed
show	floor
green	life
plant	came
hurt	sure
jump	left
please	ate

Name ______________________ Date ____________

Phonics

Final Syllables *-ent, -ant*

Circle the word that names the picture.

1.  student stable stubble	**2.**  pencil panther parent	**3.**  infant instant insist
4.  toaster talent target	**5.** 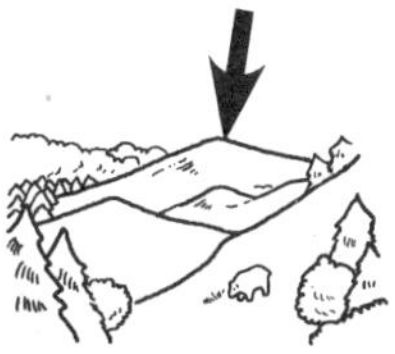 doormat distant duster	**7.**  music magnet merchant
7.  protect present pretest	**8.** 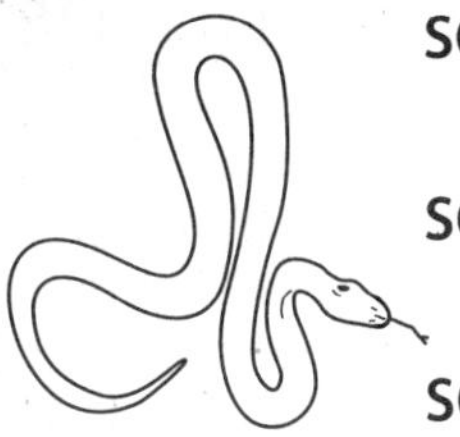 serpent servant settle	**9.**  actor agent absent
10. 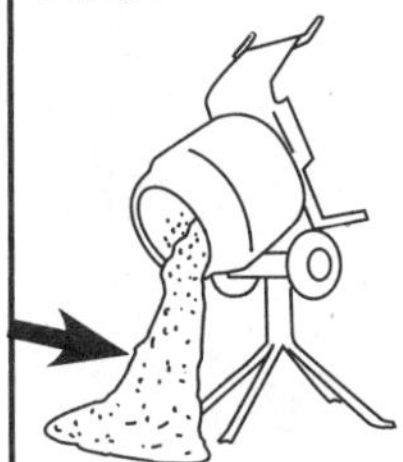 cellar constant cement	**11.**  exit event eagle	**12.**  sunset silent seven

Read It Together Are the absent students distant or in class?

Name ______________________ Date ____________

High Frequency Words

A Bed for Carla's Puppy

Write a word from the box to complete each sentence.

High Frequency **Words**
ate
bed
big
came
floor
home
left
life
new
sure

Carla got a brand ________ bed for her puppy to sleep in. She put the big bed on the ________ in her bedroom. On Tuesday morning when Carla ________ for school, the puppy was asleep in the bed. Then the puppy got hungry and ________ some of the bed. When Carla ________ back home, there was a big hole in the bed. Carla looked at her puppy and said, "You ________ are cute, but with you around, ________ will never be boring!"

Word Cards: Prepositional Phrases

across	down	off	over
through	to	toward	up
bus	desert	city	skyscraper
car	barn	road	mountain
street	log	flag	stairs
swamp	creek	gate	valley
forest	waterfall	beach	hill

Name ______________________ Date ____________

Phonics

Final Syllables *-ent, -ant*

Write the words to complete each sentence.

1. president important

I am ________ because I am the leader of a country.

I am a ________.

2. innocent infant

I am small and ________, and I need a lot of care.

I am an ________.

3. absent student

On most days I am in school, but sometimes I am

________. I am a ________.

4. parent constant

I have children who need ________ attention.

I am a ________.

5. elephant different

I am an animal that is ________ because I have a

trunk. I am an ________.

6. vacant occupant

This house is not ________ because I live in it.

I am the ________.

Name ______________________ Date ____________

Grammar and Writing

Write Prepositional Phrases

Read the story. Then choose the prepositional phrase from the box that correctly completes each sentence. Write the phrase.

on their shirts	in February	of March
on Valentine's Day	to our friends	during the year

There are many fun holidays during the year. One of them is Valentine's Day. This holiday is ______________. That is the day we give special cards ______________. Everything is red ______________. That changes just a month later on the 17th ______________. That is when we celebrate St. Patrick's Day. People wear green. They put little plants called shamrocks ______________.

Name ______________________ Date __________

Author's Purpose Chart

America Is . . .

Make an author's purpose chart. Figure out the author's purpose for writing "America Is . . ."

Clues from the Title:	**Clues from the Kind of Writing:**
"America Is . . . " The selection is about America.	Literary nonfiction presents facts and ideas in an interesting way.
Author's Purpose	
Clues from the Details:	**Clues from the Main Idea:**

Work with a partner. Compare the author's purposes that you found.

Name ______________________ Date ____________

Phonics

Syllables

Circle the word that names the picture.

1.  pencil puzzle paper	**2.** 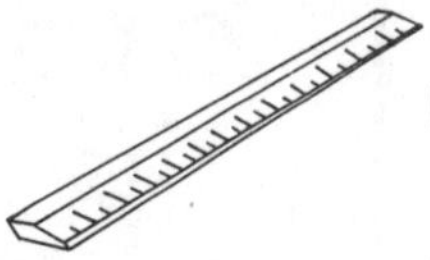 ruler rubber raisin	**3.**  caption cabin capture
4.  aside ajar asleep	**5.**  action arrive airplane	**6.**  baseball bobcat beanbag
7.  razor raindrop raccoon	**8.**  question quotation quickly	**9.** 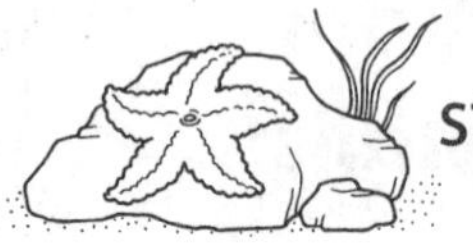 stubborn student starfish
10.  velvet vulture vacation	**11.**  address adore adult	**12.**  creatures crackles craters

Read It Together Some creatures are asleep near the cabin.

Name ______________________________ Date ______________

Phonics

Syllables

Write the words to complete each sentence.

1. **thousands jungle**

   There are __________ of plants and animals living in a rain forest __________.

2. **important reason**

   That's one __________ that these forests are __________.

3. **plants illness**

   We use some of the __________ to fight __________.

4. **location equator**

   The __________ of some rain forests is near the __________.

5. **treetops around**

   It is sunny and windy __________ the tallest __________.

6. **reptiles leafy**

   Many __________, mammals, and insects live in the __________ parts of the trees.

7. **floor biggest**

   The __________ animals live in the darkest part, on the forest __________.

Word Cards: Multisyllabic Words

 tree	 musician	 skyscraper	 circle
happiness	important	landform	explain
color	along	fly	white
fact	upbringing	duty	continent
vacation	united	bemuse	freedom
test	faithful	understand	same
compare	lot	travel	reunion

Spelling & Word Work

High Frequency Word Cards

will	man
soon	best
black	lot
brown	face
group	same
high	fly
leave	tree
study	color
open	white
point	bring

Name ______________________ Date ____________

Comparison Chart

Compare Author's Purpose

Make a comparison chart. Show how "America Is . . ." and "This Land Is Your Land" are the same and how they are different.

	"America Is . . ." by Louise Borden	"This Land Is Your Land" by Woody Guthrie
persuade readers		✓
inform readers	✓	
entertain readers		
share experiences		
express feelings		
express creativity		

Share your chart with a partner. Take turns comparing the authors' purposes in each selection.

Name ______________________ Date ____________

Phonics

Syllable Division

Divide the syllables and then circle the word that names the picture.

1.

ex|tra
ea|ger
(ea|gle)

2.

cactus
capture
cable

3.

donut
dolphin
doghouse

4.
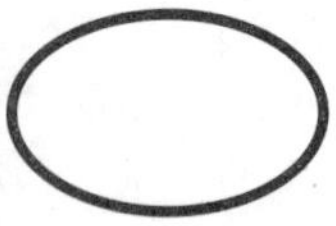
photo
oval
open

5.

menu
medal
major

7.
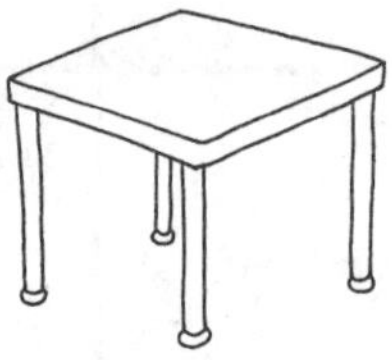
tunnel
turtle
table

7.
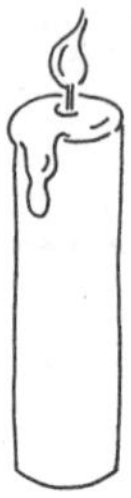
cancel
camel
candle

8.
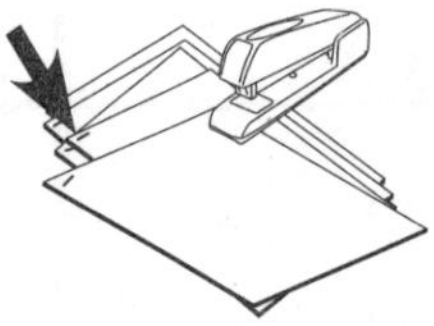
stable
stumble
staple

9.

sailfish
saddle
sandwich

10.

poodle
puddle
pebble

11.
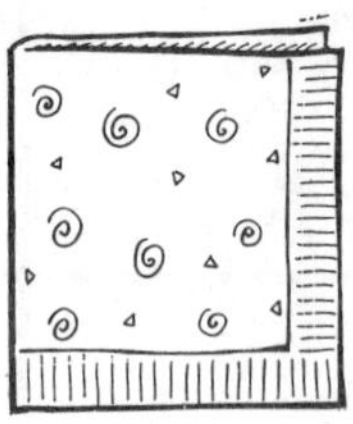
needle
napkin
nonstop

12.

lumber
little
lobster

Read It Together Do eagles, giraffes, or lobsters fly in the sky?

Name ______________________ Date ____________

High Frequency Words

An Airplane Trip

Write a word from the box to complete each sentence.

High Frequency **Words**
best
bring
color
face
fly
lot
man
same
tree
white

1. Do you go on airplane trips a ________?

2. I don't, but I will ________ on a plane today.

3. I will ________ my suitcase with me.

4. It is ________ but has splotches of a bright red color.

5. It is the ________ suitcase because it is easy to find!

6. A man with a big grin on his ________ will be waiting for me when I get off the plane!

7. When I get to Grandpa's house, I will climb the ________ to the same fort we made when I was little!

Name ______________________ Date ______________

Grammar: Prepositional Phrases

Use Prepositional Phrases

Directions:

1. Make a spinner.
2. Play with a partner.
3. First say a short sentence about America. Then spin the spinner and read the word.
4. Have your partner say your sentence with a prepositional phrase that adds more details. He or she must use the preposition you land on. Then switch roles.

Make a Spinner

1. Put a paper clip in the center of the circle.
2. Hold one end of the paper clip with a pencil.
3. Spin the paper clip around the pencil.

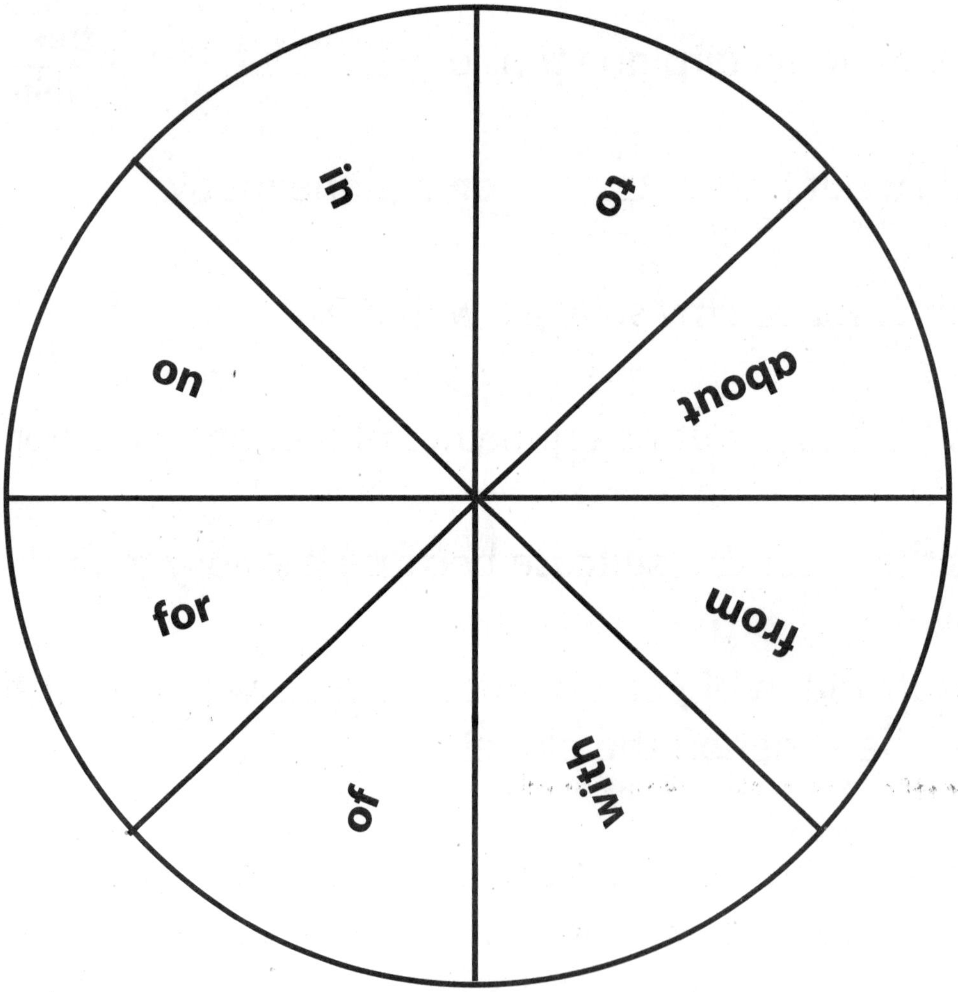

Name ______________________ Date ____________

Phonics

Syllable Division

Divide the syllables. Then write the word that completes each sentence.

1. number dolphin nature

A ________ swims in the sea, but it is a mammal.

2. hundreds candles robins

Sometimes ________ of these graceful animals swim together in a big group.

3. tiptoe open turtle

A loggerhead sea ________ swims in the sea, too.

4. simple reptile kitchen

It is a ________, not a mammal.

5. explains adults flippers

It uses its ________ to glide and steer through the water.

6. also circle recall

Sharks ________ swim in the sea, but they are fish.

7. sparkle around nation

Sharks have been ________ for a very, very long time!

8. Locate Visit Pretend

________ you are swimming in the sea. What other animals might you see?

Name ______________________ Date ______________

Grammar and Writing

Write Prepositional Phrases

Read the story. Then choose the words from the box that correctly complete each sentence.

of interesting people and places	out the door
for the National Geographic Society	during the year
about his photograph	around America

Sam Abell travels around America taking pictures. He may visit many different states ______________________. His pictures include many different subjects. They are photos ______________________. He provides photos ______________________. Here is what Sam Abell says ______________________: "It's what gets me ______________________."

Name ______________________________ Date ______________

Grammar: Prepositional Phrases

Use Prepositional Phrases

1. Partner 1 points to a sentence.
2. Partner 2 points to a prepositional phrase.
3. If the cards make a clear sentence, color in the squares. If not, begin again.
4. Play until all the squares are colored.

Sentences

Sentence Starters			
We go ________.	Teresa and I write ________.	Koji and Lynn have fun ________.	You and I read ________.

Prepositional Phrases			
to the park	after breakfast	during the concert	into the monument
along the coast	with the map	about American history	under the blue sky